WILLIAM VINCENT WALLACE

A Vagabond Composer

by Robert Phelan

Published by:
Celtic Publications
34 Ferndale
Waterford, Eire
Telephone: (051) 73125

List of Sponsors
Adapt Marketing
Fitzgerald Insurances Ltd.
Garter Lane Arts Centre
Granville Hotel
Hooper Dolan Insurances Ltd.
Jury's Hotel, Waterford

Printed by Litho Press Co. Midleton Co. Cork

DEDICATION

*To my wife, Peg, and family,
Mary, Ann, Carol, Paul and Julie
for their encouragement and support
on the long journey to publication.*

ACKNOWLEDGEMENTS

I wish to thank many people for their help. Foremost on the list must be the staff of the Waterford Municipal Library for their continuous help, especially Richard Fennessy, Head Librarian, Catherine Moran and Walter O'Neill. The staff of the National Library of Ireland, especially Phil McCann, and of Trinity College Library, were very helpful. The staff of the magnificent Reading Room of the British Museum were very tolerant of my lack of knowledge of how that wonderful institution works, and deserve my thanks, as do those in the Archive Department of Covent Garden Opera House. Invaluable information was sent by the Music Division of the New York Public Library and by the Louisiana Division of the New Orleans Public Library, and I wish to thank their staff.

During my visits to London Jimmy and Una Grimes provided a home from home for me, for which many thanks. It was a thrill to meet descendants of Wallace in London where hazel and Marjorie Wallace gave me every encouragement and help. Their cousin, Carew Wallace, kindly put his researches at my disposal, and his letter from Willy Wallace was most interesting. Mr. John Carter of 'Ottocento Archivo' made available several drawings and illustrations concerning the Wallace operas.

I had read of an unpublished biography of Wallace written over many years by Perceval Graves as a labour of love. Hazel Wallace secured from her friend Dr. Betty Graves a copy of the manuscript for me in July 1993. I had already completed the Wallace story, which I had written as 'a good read' in the modern manner. The two books covered a great deal of common ground, but because Graves' had been written many years ago, its emphasis and style were completely different to mine. I included some incidents and information in my text, and I wish to give credit to Perceval Graves and thanks to Dr. Betty Graves.

A special work of thanks is due to our respected local historians Frank Heylin and Jack O'Neill for their help. My thanks to Ann Farrell who put the manuscript on disc. To Katherine Bulbulia, Jim Nolan, Maureen Walsh and many others, whose words of encouragment meant more than they realised, a sincere 'Thank You'.

Without the help of David Power I would not have met Bill Callaghan nor heard of the LITHO PRESS. Neither would I have had the pleasure of working with a gentleman who made the publishing of my first book so easy and enjoyable.

ROBERT PHELAN
September 1994

LIST OF ILLUSTRATIONS

The Quay, Waterford

WILLIAM VINCENT WALLACE

– *Early Years in Waterford* –

As Bandmaster Wallace left his home at the top of Colbeck Street, Waterford, on a bright spring morning in the year 1812, the bells of Christ Church Cathedral opposite were not ringing out their Sunday peals over the quiet city. But he did not notice, because bells of joy were ringing in his head instead. Had he not become a proud father that very morning with the birth of his baby son. It had been an anxious time for William and Elizabeth as this was her first successful pregnancy, and to have it blessed with a healthy son was a great relief to them both. As different dates have been quoted for this happy event, the following extract from the Cathedral Baptismal Register simplifies matters: 'William, the son of William and Elizabeth Wallace, born 11th March 1812. Registered 15th March 1812 by me, Richard J. Hobson, Curate'.

According to his Army records William Wallace was from Ballina, though he has been mistakenly described as a 'Scotch Bandmaster'. He was attached to the 29th Worchester Regiment, and was an excellent musician, being a virtuoso on the bassoon. He is reputed to have been the arranger for an Army band of the famous Irish tune 'The Girl I left Behind Me'; an ironic fact in view of William junior's later life. His wife was Elizabeth Dunne from Portarlington, which is not far· from Daingean, where the parents of Vincent's future wife ran a prosperous business.

Within the year the Regiment was transferred to Ballina, and in 1813 another son was born there. His only claim to fame is his name, being called Wellington after the great Irish victor at the battle of Waterloo. In the following year, 1814, was born their sister Elizabeth, soon shortened to Eliza; in time she became an opera singer and achieved a measure of fame. While in Sydney she married an Australian bass named Bushelle, but was widowed while still young, and lived her final years in Sydney until she died there in 1878. It was while living in Ballina that Wallace first showed signs of the asthma that continually troubled him for he remainder of his life.

By the age of seven the boy's musical ability was already apparent, and he was soon proficient on the piano and clarinet. In 1825 the

Regiment was back again in Waterford where these talents could be better nurtured. As well as the invaluable example and teaching given him by his capable father, the boy was taught by Otto Hamilton and John Ringwood - the organist of Christ Church Cathedral. Close to home he attended school where he successfully passed his final examinations with high credits, especially in music, of course. By the age of fifteen he was a competent organist as well as playing most instruments in the regimental band, to the delight of his father. In fact he led the band at times, which greatly pleased Sir John Buchan, Colonel of the 29th Regiment. The Colonel and his wife took a great interest in young Vincent; Mrs. Buchan gave him the use of their library, and helped him in his general education.

In his 'Guide to Waterford' the historian Egan says with reference to Vincent: 'Above all other walks of genius, it is notable, that the one along which the heaven-inspired musicians travel, awakes the genius of its children at an age earlier than any other.

'Tis ever thus in early years
Music delights the heart.'

After living in the rustic simplicity of Ballina, the boy Vincent in his teenage years must have savoured the convivial atmosphere of a larger city. Walking the mile long Quays he could see the many trading vessels at anchor along the river, tied up at the pontoons, or sailing in or out of the gushing river so aptly called by the Vikings 'The Harbour of the Sun'. He could have ventured across the river and viewed the busy scene from the misnamed Cromwell's Rock, or looked down on the city spread out before him from the heights of Mount Misery. When walking the quayside he could have seen silks, satins, wines or other delectables for the prosperous traders; banners and flags could become alive in the wind atop tall masts; strange garb and incomprehensible accents could be heard and seen; dark skinned and weather-beaten sailors could stir the imagination with pictures of sunny vistas to be seen, delights to be sampled, exotic places to be explored and adventures to be endured. It was a historical city as witnessed by its narrow streets, the extensive remains of the city ramparts and their watch-towers, and many Churches of ancient lineage and different faiths. And welcoming every seafarer, like a latter-day Colossus of Rhodes, stood the massive bulk of Reginald's Tower, a thousand year link with the Norse invaders of old.

Across Cathedral Close from the Wallace home the skyline was dominated by Christ Church Cathedral, and this also had a foreign connection. A young Waterford man, of Welsh origin, was studying to be an architect in London, a most suitable place with its inexhaustible collection of historical and impressive buildings. After returning John Roberts was even more impressed by a beautiful girl named Mary Susanna Souchette, and they fell in love. Her father, the leader of a group of French Huguenot settlers, bitterly opposed the union, and disinherited his only daughter when they eloped and later married. They lived in Patrick Street, and had a large and happy family.

A French friend of her family, Richard Chevenix, was appointed Church of Ireland Bishop of Waterford. His predecessor, Bishop Este, had started to build a new Bishop's Palace, designed by Richard Castle, on a site overlooking the newly laid out Mall. Built of cut limestone its Doric centre-piece and arched niche above, is typical of Castle's ornate designs. But the Bishop died in 1845 with the work incomplete. Bishop Chevenix put Roberts in charge of completing the building, and was very pleased with the result. Some years later when Bishop Chevenix decided his church needed replacing, the plans of John Roberts were accepted, and he set to work. In 1793 the old medieval building was demolished, with only the crypt being retained; over the next six years an impressive Cathedral in a late Georgian Classical design took its place, with a tall spire tapering loftily into the heavens, being added in 1860.

These two impressive buildings dominated the skyline along the Mall, and perhaps caused the city fathers to redress the situation. The Mayor and Burgesses of Waterford commissioned Roberts to build an Exchange and Assembly Rooms; their civic pride had to be upheld. They must have felt proud of 'the fine building with its sequence of arched windows, set in arches of a similar kind which blended with the delicate graces of the Cathedral and Palace behind.' all of these prestigious buildings were within a stone's throw of the Wallace home, and have stood the test of time all being still in use.

The 29th Regiment was transferred overseas to the Seychelles, but William bought himself out of the Army. In the Army records there is an entry: 'April 14th 1826; Sergeant Wallace, bandmaster, was discharged on payment of twenty pound'. Posterity owes him a wealth of gratitude for this decision, made for the sake of his health, or, as seems more likely, for the sake of his son's obvious musical future. In the year

1827 the family made a wise move to Dublin, where William Wallace and his son Wellington joined the Adelphi Theatre Orchestra, the latter as a flautist. Vincent became second violin under James Barton in the Theatre Royal Orchestra. This was either a stroke of luck or of genius on Vincent's part, as the same Barton had been the teacher of Dublin born Michael Balfe. It is strange indeed that this man should have been the teacher of Balfe and Wallace, both of whom were later to become the twin pillars of British opera for the greater part of the nineteenth century.

CHAPTER TWO

– *Off to Dublin* –

To a large extent, Dublin was Ireland; certainly that was the view of the important people who lived there. Everything that mattered was controlled from within 'The Pale', the area that surround Dublin and the members of the British establishment resided within easy reach of it. Since the Irish Parliament and Trinity College were close by Dublin Castle all vital decisions were deliberated and taken within that magic triangle, and all cultural and social activities emanated from there. Naturally you had to gravitate in this direction if you were an artist, musician or sculptor who wanted to progress in life.

Outside of Dublin the only entertainment of the ordinary people was folk music or traditional music in its many forms. At the beginning of the eighteenth century the most famous and greatest traditional musician was Carolan, who was born in 1670 and died in 1738, and thus spanned both centuries. In the later part of his life his fame resulted in Carolan being accepted by the sophisticated society of Dublin, and he spent a good deal of time there. Italian baroque music was then the vogue in the city, due largely to the presence of the composer Corelli, a pupil of the great Scarlatti. Carolan, who was not just a player of the harp, became enraptured with baroque music; in his later compositions he deliberately imitated their style with success. Many other European musicians displayed their talents in Dublin in the eighteenth century. The outstanding one was Handel who arrived after a very successful spell in London. Whether it was a direct commission from an Irish charity, or simply that Handel received an invitation from the Lord Lieutenant of Ireland William Cavendish to visit Dublin, he brought with him a score upon which he was working. The previous year Handel had received from Charles Jennens the makings of an oratorio, selected from Biblical texts, and he completed the score in Dublin. On 13th April 1742 THE MESSIAH was first performed at William Neal's New Music Hall in Fishamble Street, Dublin. It turned out to have been the greatest musical event ever presented in Dublin.

Though the musical tastes of Dublin people were conservative for the remainder of the century, after the year 1800 that soon changed. The English singer Mrs. Billington and Italian soprano Angelica Catalani

11

(managed by famed Dublin born tenor Michael Kelly) focussed attention on good singing. Three of Mozart's operas were performed: COSI FAN TUTTI (1811), DON GIOVANNI and MARRIAGE OF FIGARO (1819). Two of Weber's romantic masterpieces DER FREISCUTZ (1825) and OBERON (1827), the latter less than one year after its London world premiere, delighted Dublin music lovers. Contemporaneously a number of top pianists passed through; Kalkbrenner, Moscheles and Schunke in the 1820's; later, in 1840, the greatest of them all, Franz Liszt. Thus when Wallace came to Dublin it was to a city that was familiar with and appreciated the best of music and musicians, and would hardly tolerate mediocrity.

Although Vincent's versatility enabled him to play most of the instruments in the orchestra, he sought further tuition. For the piano he attended Conran and Logier; as organist he learned from Haydn Corri, the incumbent at the Pro-Cathedral; while he studied orchestration with Phelps MacDonald. During 1828 the famous soprano Madame Catalani paid two visits to Dublin that were hugely successful, and the Theatre Royal Orchestra was highly complimented by her. The following year an Italian Opera Company under signor Spognoletti played in Dublin, and Vincent led the orchestra. He was highly praised by the conductor, and received a souvenir of the visit from him. At one rehearsal Spognoletti, on his knees on the floor, said jocosely, 'A great many notes were lost - I am looking for them - perhaps we shall find them after two or three nights'. Pointedly speaking to Vincent, he said, 'Of course you did not drop any of them".

Two of Vincent's friends from his Dublin days played important parts in his later career. Heyward St. Leger wrote after Vincent's death: 'I first met him in 1830 and from his appearance he was about sixteen years of age. I well remember seeing Vincent play first fiddle and lead the Theatre Royal Orchestra, while dressed in a short jacket usually worn by boys, when Mr. Barton was ill. Yet there were many good violinists in Dublin at that time, Fallon and McIntosh in particular.' An interesting fact is tht the lessee of the Theatre Royal at that period was Alfred Bunn, who later staged two of Vincent's operas while lessee of Drury Lane Theatre, and even wrote a libretto of sorts for him. About this time Vincent made his debut as a Concert violinist in a performance of Herz and Lafont's 'Duo on Russian Airs'.

The year 1830 proved to be a turning point in Vincent's career.

In January he was appointed Organist at Thurles Cathedral, where a new organ had been installed at a cost of one thousand pounds. Though strongly recommended by Haydn Corri, this was a strange decision for two reasons: firstly he was not yet eighteen years of age, and clearly lacked experience; secondly, he was a Protestant, whose father had been a sergeant in the British army. During his time there he wrote a Grand Mass, some motets, and an 'O Salutaris' whose melody later found its way into MARITANA. He resided in a house now occupied by the Collings family in Cathedral Street, and nearby is a bridge over the fledgeling river Suir as it gently meanders on its way to meet its sister rivers, the Barrow and the Nore, in Waterford harbour. It is claimed locally that while sitting on the bridge one summer evening Vincent heard the convent bell tolling, and this provided the inspiration for the beautiful air 'Alas those chimes' in MARITANA. Perhaps, but as recounted earlier, a similar claim regarding the bells of Christ Church Cathedral, beside his home in Waterford, appears stronger.

Part of Vincent's duties involved teaching music at the Ursuline convent school beside the Cathedral to both pupils and young nuns. Amongst his pupils were two sisters named Kelly whose father had prospered in Daingean, County Offaly, before moving to Frascati, the former residence of Lord Edward Fitzgerald, in Blackrock, County Dublin. The elder sister, Jane, entered the Convent noviciate in April 1830, and was later received as Sister Vincent. These are the girls names as recorded in the convent chronicles. It is not possible to check the baptismal register in the Daingean Church as the entries for the relevant years have mysteriously disappeared. Alicia was one of Vincent's violin pupils, and they fell madly in love. The name of Vincent's 'inamorata always appears as Isabella, for some strange reason. Perhaps it was a pet-name that became permanent; it certainly sounds more romantic.

Soon there was consternation all round: to her family, as he was an impecunious musician, and such people did not become socially acceptable for another half century; to the holy nuns comprising the Ursuline community because of the 'scandal' involved and the loss of a postulant; and especially to Sister Vincent, the embarrassed sister and companion of Alicia. Vincent proved his good faith by taking instruction and becoming a Catholic. Much later he claimed that he acted under pressure, and did not understand all that was involved; he claimed the marriage invalid on this account. He took the name Vincent as his baptismal name, hoping to mollify Sister Vincent, but without success. Yet during his later life he always used the name Vincent. It also helped to avoid being confused with a Scottish composer named William Wallace.

In the letter, written in 1859 to Anna Kelly, in which he claims that he only acted under pressure, Vincent makes the extraordinary statement: 'the heart, which you first inspired in the duets of Mayseder at Frascati, remained the same, and will ever be so, if its natural impulses are not changed'. This suggests that Vincent was infatuated with both Alicia and Anna; subsequent events seem to indicate that he wed the wrong one. With understandable reluctance the Kelly family agreed to the marriage, which took place in Dublin the following year. Vincent and Alica settled down at 11, South William Street.

It was a good time for Vincent. Not alone had he gained a beautiful adoring wife, and regained his position as sub-leader of the Theatre Royal orchestra, but some of the greatest musicians in the world came to Dublin. The occasion was the Dublin International Music Festival, held to commemorate the coronation of William IV in 1832. It was held under the auspices of the Dublin Anacreontic Society, named after the ancient Greek poet Anacreon, a group which flourished for most of the eighteenth century, and whose stated aim was ' the practice and cultivation of instrumental music'. Among the most active organisers were two wealthy brothers, Henry and William Hudson, who raised a great deal of money over the years for charitable causes. Six concerts were presented, with an orchestra under the leading British conductor, Sir George Smart. Of the seventyfour musicians playing, twentytwo were from the Liverpool Philharmonic Society. The vast choir had singers from all the principal cities, and again had members from Liverpool. Composers whose music was heard were Beethoven, Haydn, Mendelssohn, Mozart and Spohr. Musicians taking part included Mori, Ries, and the legendary Paganini.

Vincent was mesmerised by this famous violinist who performed no less than four times. It is no wonder that he was, as evidenced by the review in the Freeman's Journal dated 31st August 1831. 'Then came Paganini whom all were eager to behold as the modern Orpheus ... His appearance is strikingly peculiar, with an air of sadness about him; it seems as if his soul fell upon its own mysterious melancholy. His physical configuration is equally remarkable. Tall and gaunt, his neck is long and his head large; as he stands erect, one shoulder is higher than the other, and one arm longer than the other. His frame seems fleshless as a spectre's. It is supposed that all these physical pre-dispositions have been auxiliary advantages to enable Paganini to exer-cise those wizard powers of melody with which he is evidently gifted. He touches his one stringed violin and draws from it a strain of wild and plaintive music ... While writing under the immediate influence of Paganini's music, we do not think that any eulogy of his talents we have read exaggerated their praise. He really is a prodigy.'

The final concert was on 4th September:
'Paganini appeared again .... It is impossible to hear him without delight; the most exquisite, blended with the most astonishing, abounded. To conceive that he can produce each piece from a single stringed (G string) violin is astonishing .... Such a man in his art has never been seen before, and may, perhaps, never be seen again.'

According to Heyward St. Leger again:
'Well do I remember Vincent telling me that he used to sit up all night practicing the pieces that Paganini played. After the festival concluded the violinist gave a series of concerts at which he played all his celebrat-ed variation and concertos. It was hearing Paganini perform that inspired the soul of Vincent, and he could play more of Paganini's music than anyone except, perhaps, Sivori.'

As a leading member of the orchestra, Vincent would have been closely involved with these famous musicians, and possibly met Paganini; so it is no wonder that the impressionable young musician was not just hugely influenced, but was inspired to emulate his idol. This stimulated him to really work on his violin playing, to practice far more diligently, and to further study composition. This resulted in his presenting during the following May his own Violin Concerto at a Dublin Anacreontic Society concert to an enthusiastic reception. During 1834 Wallace led the orchestra in the first performance in Ireland of Beethoven's 'Mount of Olives', and later that year in another Italian opera season.

CHAPTER THREE

– An Australian Odyssey –

Vincent's asthma problems became acute early in 1835, and medical advice dictated moving to a warmer climate. It was decided that the Antipodes was the most suitable place; little did the composer and the doctor foresee what adventures and consequences would arise from their decision. On 9 July 1835 Vincent sailed from Liverpool on the steamer 'Rachel'. That much is clear and undisputed, as is the fact that Alica accompanied him. Who else travelled with them is shrouded in mystery.

Grattan Flood makes no mention of their son, William; whether he was born before, during or after the long voyage. He just says that Vincent abandoned Alica and William in Australia. Another version suggests that Alicia and Vincent parted shortly after their arrival in Australia, and it was on her way home that she discovered she was pregnant. This implies that Vincent never saw his son, as he is reputed never to have met Alicia again. According to Grattan Flood 'his sister and her sister' travelled with them, and it has been suggested that his brother Wellington was one of the party.

The travellers arrived at Hobart in Tasmania on 31st October 1835 on the ship 'Rachel'. Two Tasmanian newspapers record the arrival of 'Mr. and Mrs. Wallace and child and Miss Kelly'. The official Tasmanian government records show the arrival of 'Mr. and Mrs. Wallace and child'; there is no mention of Miss Kelly. Neither is there mention of Vincent's sister Eliza who went with him according to Grattan Flood. In 1897 Vincent's son William, in a brief account of his father's life, states: 'he was accompanied by his wife, two of her sisters and myself (barely two years old)'. This statement fixes the date of Willy's birth at July/August 1833. It is the first mention of two Kelly sisters travelling with Vincent and Alicia, and seems to dispel the idea that his sister Elizabeth was with them. It also strengthens the theory that she was the Elizabeth who arrived with Spencer Wallace in 1836, though then listed as his niece.

Willy also states: "My father settled down first at Parramatta", and not that 'the family' settled there. This suggests that Vincent, Alicia and Willy were at Parramatta, and perhaps the Kelly sisters were elsewhere. If, as alleged, Vincent had become more than friendly with a sister of Alicia's on the long journey out, then splitting up the party on arrival would certainlu improve matters for Alicia. Given the source of this information, it seems the most likely happening, though at variance with most other versions. If we accept Grattan Flood's suggestion that on the long voyage to Hobart Vincent and his sister-in-law Anna became romantically involved, then it is quite possible that unfriendly feelings between the sisters resulted in Anna Kelly keeping her distance from the Wallaces on arrival in Hobart. Perhaps the simple explanation is that the shipping company lists were inaccurate, and so the official records also.

The sad tale of the death of the family pet, a Newfoundland dog called Boatswain, is related by Willy. The pet was a large animal "about the size of small Shetland pony" whom Willy used ride long the banks of the local river. Vincent brought Boatswain with him on a trip to New Zealand, wehre he was killed by a native spear and then cooked nad eaten by wild Maori warriors. Vincent himself was in grave danger, but was saved by the intercession of the Chief's daughter. As a grisley reminder of his escape, Vincent brought back Boatswin's skin.

Willy also tells the stroy of a typical adventure of Vinent's. With some friends he had gone to the farm of a friend about thirty miles away on the road to the Blue Mountains for a kangaroo hunt. That night a gang of Bush rangers, led by the infamous 'Soldier Jack', attacked the station to steal Mr. Roberts' thoroughbred horses, which would have enabled the gang to keep ahead of the police. Unfortunately 'Soldier Jack' picked the wrong night to pillage the farm, because the well armed gentlemen put the dastardly attackers to flight, leaving 'copious sanguinary sights.'

During the course of the assault the ladies of the house, still clad in their neighdresses, gathered in a terrible state of alarm in young Willy's bedroom. We are not told whether they were concerned about the fate of the throughbreds or fearful of 'Soldier Jack' because of "dreadful stories of his previous misdeeds," but Willy pointedly informs us that 'Soldier Jack' and his gang were eventually captured and duly hanged. No doubt everyone shared an outburst of happiness at the good news, that is excepting the hungry families of the Bushrangers, who were probably escaped 'deportees' from the old country.

The climate was greatly to Vincent's liking, and he travelled widely in the interior, improving his health. He also organised concerts in Hobart. An interesting side-light should be mentioned at this point. In a copy of 'The Critic', published in Adelaide, Australia, in 1912 on the

17

occasion of the centenary of Vincent's birth, a writer claims:

'Wallace wrote the first part of MARITANA in Norfolk, Tasmania. It is generally supposed that the opera was written in London, but a writer in 'THE CRITIC says that the famous composer was on a visit to Tasmania in order to recoup his health, and was staying at the Bush Inn in Norfolk. The present proprietor of the Bush Inn pointed out to our correspondent, Mr. T.A. Rogers, the very spot on the balcony where Wallace stood when he first commenced to score the opera. Stretching away as far as the eye can see from this spot is a magnificent panorama, and it is easy to understand how such a title as 'Scenes that are brightest' might be inspired. A few yards away from the Bush Inn lies the Derwent river, and tourists may ramble through scenery sublime and picturesque, and drink in the heavenly beauties that abound in the garden of Australia. The composer, after remaining in Tasmania for some months, set out for England via New England, and throughout the voyage worked hard on MARITANA'. While Vincent did work hard on the way home, very little of it was on MARITANA.

The Wallace family arrived in Australia in January 1836 and settled in Parramatta, about 15 miles from Sydney. It seems a strange place for an ambitious musician to live. With the lush pastures and wide open spaces so readily to hand, the growth industry of the day was sheep; firstly for their food value, and secondly for the added value of their wool. So Vincent decided to try his hand at sheep farming, possibly as a result of receiving 100 sheep in payment for concert tickets. Since there was much more physical work involved in sheep farming than Vincent was used to, he tired of this venture fairly rapidly

A more salacious version dates the sheep farming episode nearer to the end of Vincent's sojourn in Australia. This claims that Vincent's charms had caused havoc among the society ladies in Sydney, to the distress of their fathers, husbands and men friends. In a clever move, they offered to make available to Vincent a considerable sum of money, provided he took to the bush, sheep farming or otherwise. He appreciated the message, accepted the present, and accelerated off into the outback with almost indecent haste.

The Governor General of New South Wales at that time was a Limerick man, Sir Richard Bourke, with a taste for good music. When he heard of Vincent's presence in Sydney, he lent his patronage to a concert in the Royal Hotel which was attended by all the important people.

Vincent astounded the audience by playing a Piano Concerto by Herz, followed by a Violin Concerto by Mayseder; and he repeated this feat at other concerts. It was as a violinist that he became best known, earning the title 'The Australian Paganini', something that greatly pleased him. He is still credited with being 'the first outstanding instrumentalist to visit Australia'. Again under the patronage of the Governor, Vincent opened the Academy of Music at Bridge St., Sydney in 1836, before moving to bigger premises at King Street in 1838. But the initial success did not last, and the Academy closed with debts of almost two thousand pounds, a considerable sum in those days, and a situation hardly pleasing to his generous patron.

While Vincent was making the musical headlines in Sydney in February 1836, a ship, the 'James Patterson' arrived with a group of assisted or bounty emigrants from Cork. Among the emigrants listed were the following:
'Wallace, Spencer, age 41, Musician, 2 children;
Wallace, Mrs. S. age 24, wife
Wallace, Elizabeth, age 16, actress
Kelly, Charlotte, age 25, sister of Mrs. Wallace.'

They went to live at Parramata, and later at Castlereagh Street in Sydney. Spencer gave lessons on the flute and on the violin, and became leader of the Victoria Theatre Orchestra. But by 1847 he had become insolvent and then disappeared from the records, a somewhat familiar story.

This snippet of information, contained in the late Percy Graves' unpublished biography of Vincent Wallace, opens up a whole new scenario. Who was Spencer Wallace? Was he related to Vincent? If he was, in what manner? In 1836 Vincent was aged 24, his brother Wellington 23, and his sister Eliza 22. The first possibility is that he was his uncle, his father's younger brother, if we guess the father's age at about 50. If Spencer's age is correctly given as 41, his wife's age of 24 can hardly be accurate, unless she is his second wife. This might tie in with the two young children, but what about daughter Elizabeth, aged 16? Were Spencer Vincent's uncle, could it be that this girl was Vincent's sister Eliza acting as a sixteen year old? She certainly went to Australia and married there.

The fourth adult in the party is another surprise, Charlotte

Kelly, sister of Mrs. Wallace. But which Mrs. Wallace, Mrs. Spencer or Mrs. Vincent? Her age (25) would be compatible with either. We may remember that Vincent was reputed to have been very friendly with more than one of the Kelly sisters at Frascati. This he freely admits in a letter written in 1859 to Anna Kelly, then Mrs. James Jones: 'But the heart you first inspired remained the same and will ever be so'. It is possible that Charlotte is simply the sister of Mrs. Spencer Wallace and just travelled to Australia with her, but the surname Kelly is a strange coincidence, even though it is very common in Ireland.

Another possibility is that Spencer was Vincent's father. This becomes more likely if we accept the age given him, 41, as inacurate, which is quite possible in those days of incomplete documentation. If he were in his late forties, he could be father of Vincent and Elizabeth as stated. Vincent's father is always named as William, the composer as William Vincent, and his son as William also. Strangely enough, in his account of Vincent's life, William gives the composer's father's name as Spencer, the only place where this name turns up. Although in his sixties at the time, this is hardly a fact that he would get wrong; he even gives his grandmother's full name, Elizabeth Dunne. It may well be correct that Spencer is the proper name of Vincent's father; William Spencer or Spencer William.

Vincent departed from Sydney on the 'Neptune', as reported in the 'Sydney Gazette' of 17 February 1838:
'Mr. Wallace, the Australian Paganini, left the Colony in a clandestine manner, and has sailed for Valparaiso, after having contracted debts in Sydney amounting to two thousand pounds.'
The writer deplores Vincent's conduct, and suggests that the authorities in Valparaiso should be warned against a repetition of it in Chile. When the 'Neptune' called to the Bay of Islands in New Zealand, Vincent broke his voyage there, perhaps fearing arrest at the behest of his creditors.

His later movements were related by Wellington Guernsey. Of all things, he went on a whaling expedition on the ship 'Good Intent'. One night the natives among the crew mutinied, and killed all the Europeans aboard except Vincent and the cook, a Scotsman named McClelland. The latter was spared because they knew he had done his best for them; and Vincent because he had entertained them with his violin. They were abandoned in a ships boat with little food or water, and suffered greatly before landing in the wilds of New Zealand. There are different versions of the next part of the story.

The first says that they were not ill-treated by the natives, but well received. With the result that McClelland took unto himself a Maori bride, and settled down there permanently. Vincent had other ideas but after being caught flirting with the chieftain's wife, he was sentenced to death. But he was helped to escape by the chieftain's daughter, whom he had also befriended, and she procured a boat and food to enable him to escape.

In the second version, the wild Maori captured them both, and held them for the next celebratory occasion. The sight of a corpulent cook and a calorific composer stewing simultaneously over open fires was too good for even an uneducated savage to miss. The waiting may have been hard on the captive's nerves, but it saved their collective bacon. The daughter of one of the chief's fell in love with the main course for the next celebration, begged her father to save him, and secured him for herself. It is not recorded if Vincent was as pleased with his side of the bargain, but no doubt he made the most of his time there. Presumably McClelland's fate was somewhat similar.

Although more difficult to believe, the third account has more evidence to back it up. It is written later by the French composer and writer Hector Berlioz, who while working in London between 1848 and 1855 came to know Vincent very well. They spent many evenings together around a bowl of punch, Vincent telling of his strange adventures, and Berlioz listening avidly. Berlioz proved himself to be a very shrewd observer in his other writings so his assessment that the stories must be true because 'Vincent was too lazy to have invented them' must be respected. If indeed Vincent did invent the stories, he had missed his vocation, as he would have made a wonderful writer of novels or thrillers. A shortened translation of the Berlioz story tells us:

'I was in Sydney when the Captain of an English frigate, whom I knew, suggested that I go with him on a punitive expedition against the natives of Tavei-Pounamon Bay, in New Zealand. These ferocious natives had plundered a whale-boat and eaten its crew .... As we approached the Bay the Captain transformed the ship by hiding the cannons and concealing the soldiers and most of the crew below deck. Although the Maori had spotted us, their usual caution made them quiet; but on counting only a dozen men on deck, they seized their weapons, jumped into their canoes, and headed towards us. I have never seen so many canoes in my life, they came out of everywhere.. It was like a shoal of huge fish swimming by our sides and closing ranks ... When the canoes were well within range and too tightly packed to tack, the Captain shouted orders. The cannons stuck out their heads all at once, like curious people at windows, and started to pour fire at the tattooed warriors ... From the height of a spar of the mainmast, where I had climbed with my pockets full of cartridges and my double-barrelled rifle, I played my part in removing the appetite for fight of the Maori.... The sea was strewn with corpses, limbs, broken heads, paddles and bits of boats; here and there outlined in the green water were large red pools .... Two magnificent Maori chiefs were pulled out of the water half dead, but after an hour the two Goliaths stood upright as vigorous as panthers. Our interpreter reminded them of the fate of the whalers, and told them that we had come to avenge them, but that whites did not kill their prisoners.

When the Captain informed us that he had to go to Tasmania, the ship's surgeon expressed a desire to stay on in order to study the flora of New Zealand, providing he was picked up after the ship had returned to Sydney. When this was agreed, the idea of studying these natives caught hold of me, and I offered to join the surgeon. We offered to grant the two Chief's their liberty in return for their guarantee of our safety, and they agreed. I felt a certain tightness of heart as I set foot on the now deserted beach, as our only safeguard was the dubious word and authority of the two Chiefs. On meeting their people, they explained that a pact had been made, and that they owed their freedom to us. We were then made kneel before the assembly, and a ritual was performed which made us sacrosanct.

I had learned some words of the Kanak language which is spoken in Tahiti as well as New Zealand, and I used this to seduce two charming Maori girls. They were as charming as grisettes in Paris, with beautiful eyes and eye lashes as long as fingers. Once tamed, they followed me like llamas; Mere carried my shotgun and powder bag; Maranga carried all the game that I shot; and they slept with me alternately. 'What night, what stars, what sky! It was paradise on earth! ...

Some time later I was hit by the most unexpected and infernal of sorrows. Emai, my chief protector, had a daughter, Tatea, whose piercing beauty plunged me into the depths of a terrible love when I saw her. Her father took warmly to my interest, but she resisted obstinately. I had gone off the other two girls, and I wanted, after a few tender words, to lead Tatea down into a field of phorum, the flax of the country. I offered her many gifts, and even threatened to cut off my little finger, but nothing worked. I stopped eating, sleeping, smoking: I no longer hunted or even spoke to my two girls. They too were crying and unhappy, and tried to change Tatea's mind, as jealousy is thought absurd in New Zealand. Finally I got an idea; to offer Tatea the barrel of tobacco and pipe which I always carried on my back. The most consoling of smiles welcomed my offering, which she accepted: she was overjoyed to possess the precious barrel that she had coquettishly refused to seek. When she gave me her hand I thought I could feel my heart melt, and Tatea untied her hair and led me, palpitating, towards the field of phorum. 'My dear follow, don't speak to me of European women!' ...

Shortly afterwards the surgeon returned from his botanical exploration covered in plants and looking like a walking haystack. Our Chiefs decided to celebrate this reunion and my marriage with a splendid feast. They had just caught a young slave in the act of stealing in their village, and decided to kill him for this solemn occasion. When I was offered the shoulder of the slave, I found it impossible to touch, which offended the Chiefs. Out of bravado the surgeon tried to taste the shoulder, but was immediately violently sick. This greatly annoyed the cook Koro, whose pride was wounded, but the Chiefs and Tatea calmed him by praising his cooking to the heights.

I had forgotten England and the world, when the frigate reappeared to remind me that there was somewhere else calling me. At first Tatea seemed resigned, but when the ship's boat came ashore, and the surgeon had boarded it she threw herself at my feet distraught. Seizing a knife from her father, she scarred my chest with two strokes, and threw herself on top of me to cover herself with my blood as proof of her love ... I had left Tatea in a faint on the shore, and when I reached the ship's ladder, I saw at my feet in the water my two girls Mere and Maranga swimming with one hand and making farewell gestures and wailing 'O Walla, O Walla' - that was how they pronounced my name. After reaching the deck, I was about to jump back into the water, but the Captain prevented me.

I rushed into a cabin and collapsed, lying there like a living corpse for hours, without drink or food. When I came to my first act was to rush up on deck, but we were already far away - there was nothing only sky and water. My chest was still bleeding, so wishing to make the scar permanent, I procured some gunpowder and coral, mixed them carefully, and applied a poultice to the wound. Chief Emai had taught me this method of tattooing, and it succeeded perfectly.

Berloiz commented: 'At this point Vincent then opened his shirt and showed me a large blue cross engraved on his chest. I would give a lot to know if that tattoo on his chest is still visible. That night I reflected on the hospitality of the New Zealanders, the frenzied patriotism of the English, the influence of small kegs of tobacco, and on savage love and polygamy'.

CHAPTER FOUR

– *The Happy Wanderer* –

Instead of settling down after these adventures - like any good composer - Vincent continued his travels; he later gave an elaborate account of his journeys in an American paper interview in 1842. After his New Zealand odyssey he landed in the Indian city of Madras. He spent some months at the court of the Begum Queen of Oudh, becoming a great favourite of hers, and being rewarded with diamonds and rubies. Another patron was a Rajah, whose guests Vincent entertained, musically of course. But life was never hum-drum for Vincent, and while on a tiger hunt with the Rajah he was nearly killed. A huge tiger leaped suddenly from the undergrowth and knocked him from his horse. Luckily Vincent had the presence of mind to retrieve his rifle and fire into the tiger's face as it leaped again and landed on top of him, fracturing some of his ribs. Two of the Rajah's wives nursed and comforted Vincent during his recovery from his injuries.

An even more colourful account of this story appeared in 'The Theatre' in 1864 in an inaccurate account of his life. This time it happened while Vincent was guest of an Army Regiment at Simala in India. When out hunting alone and on foot, he was confronted suddenly by a tiger. As the animal leaped Vincent fired his rifle and wounded it in the shoulder. When the tiger rushed at him Vincent, though lacerated by its claws, succeeded in dispatching him with his hunting knife. His Army friends considered his coolness an courage deserving of commemoration, so they presented Vincent with a gold watch inscribed with his name and date and the place of his escape.

An incident with a tiger in the wilds of India would not seem material for an opera libretto, but that is reckoning without Vincent's perspicacity. His last opera THE DESERT FLOWER is set among the American Indians who lived by hunting. The tribe's cheiftainess, Pocohontas of the original story but now called Oanita, is in love with the dashing Captain Maurice. No doubt wishing to impress his beloved Maurice sings:

Through the pathless forest drear,
See the hunter threads his way,
His dauntless breast ne'er knoweth fear,
As forth he goes in search of prey.

Hist, the tiger leaves his lair,
His flashing eyes with fury burn,
Quick then, hunter, load with care,
Mark him ere he this way turn!

He sees me now, and with swift spring,
Yes, hither he prepares to bound,
Take steady aim; the echoes ring,
Huzza, he's lifeless on the ground.
Ah no other life, no pastime fair
Can with the Hunter's joys compare.

Oanita must have been suitably impressed, because they faced death together before LOVE'S TRIUMPH, the name of another of Vincent's operas. Unfortunately the same impression was not made on the London music lovers, because the opera did not last long.

The watch, said to have been given at Simla, leads to another typical story about Vincent. When in Europe years later he went to the Mediterranean on a yacht with friends. Vincent left his watch in a locker when they landed on a small island for a day's shooting. When the party returned to the beach where the yacht had been lying at anchor, the vessel was no longer there; it was never again heard of or seen. It was presumed that the Greek crew plundered all the property on board and scuttled the boat. Some year later in Paris an acquaintance of Vincent's told him of seeing in the window of a jeweller's shop a watch inscribed 'Wallace'. Vincent went to the shop, recognised the watch as his own, and bought it from the astonished jeweller. The latter explained that he had purchased it from a Jewish pedlar, who had bought it with other jewellery from a Greek sailor in Genoa. Vincent was thrilled to get back his watch for its own sake, not to mention the fact that it was now a conversation piece, and wore it for many years.

Just as the story of the tiger attack appeared in different versions, so too with the presentation watch. Willy Wallace relates the story as happening off the coast of Chile, after Vincent met an old friend whom he had met in Australia, in Havanna and now again in Vaparaiso. They were on board ship travelling back to 'centres of civilisation' and Vincent had with him a chest containing all his valuable curiosities and possessions. A fierce storm caused the ship to shelter in a small coastal town, and Vincent and his friend Dr. Martyn wined and dined until after dark, only to then discover that no local boatman would brave the rough seas to return them to their sailing ship. They were forced to spend the night ashore, and in the morning were dispmayed to see that the ship had set sail without them, carrying on board Vincent's possessions. The vessel was neither seen nor heard of again.

Ten years later Vincent was holding forth while dining with friends in the Astor Hotel in New York. When he had related the story of the tiger and the watch one of the genlemen said: "Well Mr. Wallace, I guess I saw the identical watch, or one uncommonly like it, in the window of a watchmaker's down Boston way.' He gave Vincent the name and address of the shop, and in due course the identical watch arrived back, to the astonishment of Vincent and his impressed friends. The watchmaker's explanation was that he had bought it among other articles from a seafaring man some months previously. As Willy remarked: "the sea sometimes gives up its dead, but this was the first occasion it had given up a presentation watch."

Vincent was again bitten by travel-lust, and he sailed on one of the flying clippers across the vast expanse of the Pacific ocean to South America. On his arrival at Valparaiso in Chile, he found an active and influential British colony which welcomed him. Vincent first performed in a concert there on 3 June 1838, and others followed, some in Santiago. While in this city he was reminded of a concert scheduled for the next day 125 miles away in Valparaiso which had slipped his mind. Rather than break his word, to the Sisters of Charity, Vincent rode the journey in eleven hours, and using thirteen horses, to get to the venue. It would be interesting to read how he performed at the concert, and what kind of reception was accorded him, as no doubt the details became known.

Among the fellow artists that performed with Vincent was a Paris born pianist named Barre, which had arrived in Chile in 1824 after studying at the Paris Conservatoire. He spent thirty years teaching on the piano in Chile, and also composed. Another performer was the Chilean born composer Jose Zapiaola, best known for a patriotic march in praise of a Chilean victory over Peru at the battle of Yungay in 1838. An old Spanish harper named Pasquita Robles added to the entertainment, as did a nameless young Scotsman who sang his native folk songs.

Next Vincent crossed the majestic cordilleras of the Andes on his way to Buenos Aires in Argentina. When we realise that there were no railways in those places at that time, and that the arduous journeys had to be done on foot, horse and mule, it is an extradordinary feat by a man said to be in indifferent health all his life. Since there was a war on with France when he arrived, the locals had more than music on their minds, so his visit was fruitless. Back across the continent he travelled to Santiago, where a number of profitable concerts improved his bank balance and his spirits. Here Vincent is said to have had a repeat of his Australian experience with the sheep; this time some local music lovers parted with their prize fighting cocks in payment for a concert, so great was their devotion to the Muse. Another passing event was an earthquake that he survived, while getting caught up in a local war on the borders between Chile and Peru was just a diversion. But it was not all excitement and hardship; he is said to have pocketed over 5,000$ for one concert.

This time Vincent headed northwards to Lima in Peru, where he was again made welcome and feted. It seems that the people of South America inspired Vincent to give of his best, and some of his greatest successes, artistically and financially, took place there. He visited Panama, Jamaca and Cuba, giving concerts in the principal cities.

After arriving in Mexico City early in 1841 Vincent quickly settled in, and conducted a season of Italian opera there to much acclaim. He travelled to Tampico and Veracruz for successful concerts. Vincent composed a Grand Mass and conducted it; no trace of it has been found perhaps because it was an enlarged version of the Mass that he had composed as a young man in Thurles. It could have been his obituary, as the Spanish Inquisition was still active in Mexico, and it turned its attention to him. Because he was no longer a practicing Catholic, and was well known for his extravagant lifestyle, he was at risk. When friends tipped him off to the danger, Vincent declined to face an altogether more dangerous tiger, and beat a hasty retreat. Ringing in his ears was the accolade 'A virtuoso of the first rank' given him by the Mexican music lovers.

The new Mexican President, Santa Anna, was very fond of music and Vincent and he became close friends. As the country was in an unstable state politically, Santa Anna frequenly had to resort to arms to maintain his position and naturally Vincent had to be part of the excitement. In one of these battles Santa Anna was defeated, and when Vincent was lfeeing for his life his horse was shot from under him. The old Mexican soldier who was guiding him put Vincent on his own horse and told him to gallop on as fast as he could. As he hurried off, Vincent looked back and saw the Mexican shoot the first fugitive to approach him, without checking whether he was friend or foe, and appropriate his horse. Vincent flet sure the man was one of their own, but he did not stop to ask any questions.

One morning Vincent was walking in Mexico city holding a large white umbrella to protect him from the blazing sun. Three drunken soldiers on guard duty decided the umbrella would be an excellent target, and proceeded to shoot it to bits. Fortunately Vincent was not hit, and the noise of the affray drew to the scene some officers whom he knew, and the position was explained to them. A drumhead court martial was held, and within a couple of hours of the shots being fired, the three soldiers were lined up against a wall for execution. Vincent pleaded with Santa Anna for their lives, but he insisted on executing them as an example to other indisciplined soldiers.

Wallace's next journey was a short one, just across the Gulf of Mexico to New Orleans. Centre of the French efforts to colonise the Americas, New Orleans was a thriving cosmopolitan city in close and regular contact with Paris. Given the large number of French cognostici who cherished their erudition and taste, Wallace could hardly fail to attract attention. How he succeeded is graphically related in the biography of the famous American concert pianist Louis Moreau Gottschalk.

'The most memorable event in the musical history of New Orleans that season, (a season that had already seen the production of Meyerbeer's LES HUGENOTS and the world premiere of Prevost's LA ESMERALDA), was the coming of William Vincent Wallace. He arrived on New Year's Day 1842 on a small sailing vessel, which he had boarded at Vera Cruz. He landed with a violin and little else. There was not a person in New Orleans whose name he knew, and not one had ever heard of him.

He spent the night in a cheap hotel in the American faubourg. The next morning he chanced to see in a newspaper the announcement of a concert of sacred music to be given that evening at Dr. Clapp's church. An hour before the concert was due to begin he was at the church with his violin. He introduced himself to the choir director, played for him on both the violin and the piano, and asked permission to appear in just one short number on each instrument at the end of the scheduled programme. The choir director, almost overcome by the stranger's virtuosity whether as pianist or violinist, unhesitatingly granted the request. The audience that night had no notion of leaving after hearing the unexpected artist in two short numbers. Wallace, now at the piano, and now with his violin, was called back again and again, each time to play one of his own compositions. The next day all new Orleans was talking about the magic of 'the vagabond Irish music-maker'.

'Moreau was introduced to him the following Sunday night at Madame Boyer's. The boy expected to see someone resembling one of Ossian's bards; instead he met a gentleman, correctly groomed. Wallace played that night three pieces he had just composed, with Moreau reading at sight from the manuscript, accompanying him. The visitor next improvised on the piano, developing themes suggested by the audience. He then sang, to his own accompaniment, half a dozen songs for which he had written both words and music. Long before the last one ended, half the group in the drawing room were in tears. This man, thought Moreau, embodied melody. No one like him had ever before been heard in America. His music was altogether different from the French and Italian music with which New Orleans was familiar. His tunes captured the listeners heart and held it. As Moreau watched him play and sing, he suddenly recalled the story of the pact between Paganini and the Devil. It appeared that there was also a pact between Wallace and some supernatural creature. But it could not be a creature out of Hell, reasoned the boy. Years later he was to say: 'I actually found myself looking sharp, half expecting to see the tips of two folded white wings protruding below Wallace's long black coat'.

'The extraordinary personal history of the Irish musician was soon known to most of those present at Madame Boyer's ... After arriving in Australia he tried to break away from the spell of the violin and the piano, and settled down on a farm and raised sheep. But the urge to make music was too compelling. To his wife, who refused to leave the farm, he gave his last shilling, and then took to the open sea ...

'Scarcely a week passed during that winter and spring when the visitor did not make three or four public appearances. He played in theatres, ballrooms, lodge halls and churches, on both the violin and piano and always his own music. The New Orleans printer who contracted to publish his more popular compositions found it hard to supply the demand for his polkas, schottisches, waltzes and quadrilles. No one in New Orleans was to be surprised at the immediate and astounding success of his opera MARITANA when produced at Drury Lane, London in 1845.'

'Moreau played with Wallace many times in the Gottschalk home, at Madame Boyer's, at Monsieur Letellier's in Felix Miolan's studio, and elsewhere. Wallace spoke of the boy as 'the American Franz Liszt', although he was only thirteen years of age. Moreau could not then have dreamed to what extent his own musical ideas were to agree with Wallace's. A strong friendship sprang up between man and boy, one that was to endure throughout the years, as we shall see later.'

'Wallace also found time to conduct opera at the Theatre d'Orleans, whose musical director, Monsieur Prosper Prevost, (the composer?), was quoted in a local paper:
'Wallace was so much cheered by these French artists that they laid down their instruments and abandoned the tutti to applaud le jeune Irelandais'. Unfortunately Wallace contracted swamp fever there, and spent some months recuperating in the country before returning in November for a farewell concert that was packed out, and he went happily on his way to the real America.'

Where Vincent went, when he left the steamy damp atmosphere of New Orleans, is in doubt. One place mentioned is the State of Montana, and if this is correct, a strange co-incidence ensues. Montana is way out west in the lower reaches of the Rocky mountains, almost as remote and far from Waterford as you could get. Yet over the next twenty years a large colony of men and women from 'The gentle county' were to settle there.

During Vincent's youthful days in Waterford the most prosperous part of County Waterford was the area along the coast around Bunmahon. In this countryside there were extensive deposits of copper and zinc, and mining gave great employment locally. At the height of the operations there, over 1,000 people worked in different sections, a huge number in those times. The moving spirit behind this operation was Thomas Wyse, who was also instrumental in providing badly needed employment in the Portlaw area with his smelting mill at Pouldrew. Most of the raw material used in the mill came from the Bunmahon mines. Sadly the death of Thomas removed the fulcrum of the operation, and when the world price of copper plummeted to uneconomical levels, the copper mines were closed down. The hundreds of skilled miners had no choice but to emigrate to find work, and most of them became miners in the newly found deposits in Montana.

Nor is that the only link, for some years later another of Waterford's famous sons, Thomas Francis Meagher played his part in setting up the new state government. Meagher was born in the present day Granville Hotel, on the centre of the Quay in Waterford. His father had been Mayor of the city, and Thomas quickly espoused the cause of nationalism while at college. He supported the 1848 Rebellion, and used his talents as a journalist and orator to further the cause. This attracted police attention. Imprisoned and deported for his republican activities and writings, Meagher was deported to Tasmania (another co-incidence with Vincent). After some years there he escaped and made his way to America, and became a Brigadier of the famous fighting 69th Regiment. He led his company in many famous battles, including Frederickburg. It was after this battle at Mayer's Heights (better known as 'Bunker Hill'), that General Robert E. Lee said of the Irish Brigade: 'Never were men so brave. They ennobled their race by their splendid gallantry on that desperate occasion.'

After the end of the Civil War the task of reorganising the destitute and law-less areas of the country posed great problems, so a man with Meagher's proven ability and talents was invaluable. He was appointed Acting-Governor of Federal Territory of Montana by the Republican President Abraham Lincoln, and he was effectively running the Territory during the regular absences of Governor Syndey Edgerton in Washington. Facing strong opposition from well organised Southern Democrats, not to mention the Klu Klux Klan, with armed bands of outlaws scouring the countrysdie and displaed Indian tribes attacking settlers, Meagher was, in his own succinct phrase, "Commander, not of an invincible, but invisible army."

On the 1st July 1867 Meagher arrived at Fort Benton, on the upper Missouri river, exhausted after spending six days riding over 200 miles from Virginia City. Despite his position of authority and the obvious danger from outlaws, roaming Indians, or just plain killers, no accommodation was offered at the Army camp, so he stayed on a river-boat, the G.A. Thompson. About 10 p.m. a noise was heard near his cabin, followed by a splash. A quick search revealed that the guard-rail outside the cabin was broken or missing, and nothing to be seen except the dark rushing river, as there were few lanterns on the boat or the levee. Meagher had disappeared into the night and not a trace of him was ever found. Inevitably foul play was suspected: why was no accommodation available for the Acting Governor in the army camp in such dangerous times ? ; and why was no guard posted outside the ship's cabin as a precaution. The State of Montana was the poorer for the loss of so capable an administrator as Meagher at the tragically early age of 44, murdered by the Klu Klux Lkan.

Inevitably Vincent now made his way towards the cities on the east coast of America, spending time in Philadelphia in 1842, before moving to Boston the following year. The roving musician was accepted with alacrity, and he was soon immersed in concert work and teaching. During the winter of 1843 the Boston Music Festival attracted leading musicians. Among them were three of the most celebrated violinists in the world, the two Belgians, Artot and Veiuxtemps, and Ole Bull from Norway. Strong competition indeed, but Wallace was not found wanting. A report in a Boston paper says: "These are three of the most renowned violinists in the world; but Wallace maintained his ground'. His 'piece de resistance' was his own Introduction and Variations entitled LA CRACOVIENNE."

In a review, 'The Athenaem' of London reported:
'Artot is one of the foremost and elegant violinists of the Rubini school: he is also one of the handsomest, and is beloved for his amiability and gentleness.
Bull is fashioned in the heroic mould; he is Norse to his backbone, and is consumed with the love of his native land. He is a natural genius, and practically self-taught. He used mostly his own compositions.
Wallace is too fond of parading his own music, and goes in for virtuosity and display rather than content'.

During the years 1842 and 1843 he must have also spent some time in New York. Amazingly, there was no association of professional musicians nor any complete orchestra in that city ' capable of performing the grand instrumental compositions of the great masters'. At last Urelli Corelli Hill assumed the responsibility of calling a meeting, and of notifying the musicians of the city of it, at the Apollo Rooms on Saturday 2nd April 1842. This meeting established the Philharmonic Symphonic Society of New York, and among its founder members was Wallace. At the first concert given at the Apollo rooms on 7th December 1842, the programme consisted of:

Beethoven	Symphony in C	cond. U.C. Hill
Weber	Ov. Oberon	cond. D.G. Etienne
Kelliwoda	Overture in D	cond. H.C. Tinans

The orchestra consisted of 75 members; 53 were active Professors of Music, and the remaining 23 were professional musicians. It was ahead of its time by being run on a profit-sharing basis. The roster of players during the first season has long since disappeared, but Krehbiel, in a commemoration of the 50th Anniversary of the Society, gives the names of 65 players during the second season. Among the list is: Pianoforte and Violin: W. Wallace.

The earlier programmes were enlivened by programme notes which now seem to articulate good-will rather than musicology. We read that "the story of ORPHEUSE E ERUDICE was the inspiration for Beethovan's 7th Symphony; that his EROICA contains French republican airs; that the auditor of Mendelssohn's MIDSUMMER NIGHT'S DREAM, if he gives a little scope to his imagination, while still keeping the play in his memory, may fancy himself dreaming."

In June 1843 there is a comment in the New York Herald concerning Vincent Wallace:
'Quite a young man of modest and unpretending demeanour, he is full of enthusiasm and is a tremendous success. He performed his own composition, Introduction and Variations on 'La Cracovienne', on the piano and on the violin.'
The concert was repeated in Boston and Philadelphia.

The New York Mirror carried another report:
'New York is alive with a new musical prodigy, Vincent Wallace. There is no doubt tht he is the best pianist ever heard in this country'. In December 1843 a concert was held in the Tabernacle, a Church cum Concert Hall, with a capacity of 2,000 people, and a very popular venue. Ole Bull was the violinist, Vincent the pianist, and Madame Otto the soprano soloist; and the hall was packed.

We have this contemporary description of Vincent by his friend

Wellington Gourney, who was his companion through many a long journey:
'He was slim and always carefully and elegantly dressed. There was high intelligence in his face, but it lacked fire; there was a dreamy languorous look about him. He was always romantically linked with half a dozen romances. Vincent was an exemplary man, a most affectionate parent, and a warm hearted hospitable friend. We shall rarely see his equal."

Young Wallace

35

There is also a fine pencil sketch of vincent drawn by the Bavarian artist Juan Mauricio Rugendas. This was drawn for his patron Senora Isodora Zegeras de Huneeus a rich Chilean lady, whose salon was a regular calling place for Vincent while in that country. It is a fine head and shoulders portrait of a young man with a high forehead, an abundance of dark curly hair, a quizzical expression, and intense eyes that grab the attention.

Life was going so well for Vincent that he had accumulated a good deal of money, an unusual situation for him. He invested in a furniture and piano making business. But his business acumen did not match his musical expertise, or perhaps he was gullible to American salesmanship, for by 1844 his investment had disappeared. A series of farewell concerts helped redress the position, and he was happy to leave the hustle and bustle of the New World behind him and go back to Europe. After a brief stop in London Vincent embarked on a concert tour of Germany and Holland, and stored up memories and ideas that were later to prove useful in the settings of hiw operas. But London was calling, and Vincent was now prepared to listen.

CHAPTER FIVE

London at Last

Early in 1845 Vincent made his entrance upon the London musical scene as a pianist at a concert starring Signor Marras, one of the principals at the Italian Opera Company, at Covent Garden on 8 May 1845. This concert at the Hanover Square Rooms, saw Vincent as piano soloist in two of his compositions: Grand Fantasia and Variations on romance from the opera L'ECLAIR and Variations and Scherzo on LA CRACOVIENNE. Marras sang the aria 'LE REVE' by Vincent, and the critic J.W. Davison commented: 'Nothing could have been more delicious than his manner of rendering of the charming 'Reve' of Mr. Wallace.' Of the concert in general the 'Musical World' critic had this to say:

'The great feature of this concert was the debut of Wallace, a pianist and composer of distinguished ability ... As a pianist Wallace is not a Leopold de Meyer, nor is he a Mendelssohn; ...that he is an admirable pianist there can be little doubt ..... He has a firm touch, a brilliant finger, a finished mechanism and a fund of sentiment and grace. If these are

Wallace by J. Hanshew (Nat. Gallery of Ireland)

not enough to constitute him a pianist of high rank, what else is required?'

But as Professor Dent has pointed out, from 1830 to 1860 England was not regarded abroad as a musical country. Neither was it considered capable of producing serious musicians and composers. So it became a happy hunting ground for foreign musicians and singers. Again Dent says: 'That a gentleman should become a professional musician remained utterly unthinkable until about the end of the Victorian era.' Thus such famous pianists as Clementi, Moscheles, Sterndale Bennett and Thalberg played and taught in London for many years.

Whether Wallace's arrival in London at this particular time was another stroke of good luck, or a shrewd move on his part, is debatable. For a number of reasons the timing was to his advantage. Over a long period of years the English musical public has been given a surfeit of foreign opera; German opera was predominant at first, but then gave way to Italian 'Bel Canto'. A section of music lovers, and many British musicians and composers, felt that an English opera company could and would gain support. Several British composers had operas produced with at least some degree of success, the more prominent being Barnett, Bishop, Loder and Macfarren. But no breakthrough was made.

Then came Michael Balfe, Dublin born and trained, but with years of experience behind him in European opera houses. He was an excellent singer, holding his place on the European stage for about fifteen years. His early operas were written and produced in Italy, where he learned his trade thoroughly. By 1835 he was confident enough in his abilities to face the home audiences, and THE SIEGE OF ROCHELLE was successfully performed at Drury Lane. He even sang the leading baritone role. In the following year Drury Lane staged his next opera THE MAID OF ARTOIS, which Balfe wrote specially for Europe's leading soprano Malibran with whom he frequently sang. Seven years later he wrote the opera that is forever linked with his name, THE BOHEMIAN GIRL, and it too was produced at Drury Lane. It was the most successful English opera ever written, even appearing later in an Italian setting as LA ZINGARA. So the stage was set for Wallace.

In London Vincent was living at 87 Piccadilly, over a music shop owned by a Russian called Baron Wykoff. He it was who published the first of Vincent's many piano pieces such as 'Le Chant d'Amour', 'La Gondola', 'Le Reve' and 'Le Zephyr'. At one of Vincent's concerts St.

Leger was impressed not only by Vincent's style of dressing but also by his compositions. He brought Vincent to the house of Edward Fitzball, the most accomplished English librettist of the day, and introduced them. Vincent played 'La Gondola' and other compositions, and Fitzball was immediately enchanted by what he heard. As he related in his autobiography: 'When Wallace sat down and gave me a taste of his quality I was deeply impressed. He was a magnificent pianist, and played to me the splendid composition 'The Harp in the air', to which I wrote the words and which has become very popular.

Fitzball was sufficiently confident of Vincent's ability that he gave him the first Act of a libretto on which he was working, and which turned out to be MARITANA. Fredrick Beale, the leading London music publisher, had been impressed by Vincent's concert pieces, and

MARITANA at Drury Lane

when he heard that he was working on an opera, Beale called to his house. He was a good judge of what would sell, and when Beale heard Act 1, which was all that had been completed, he bought the rights to the whole of MARITANA on the spot.

In an-other coincidental happening, an old acquaintance of Vincent's from his years in Dublin now enters the story. Alfred Bunn was lessee of Drury Lane Theatre, but was at first reluctant to stage the work. It took some time to persuade him to change his mind; perhaps it was only when Fitzball and Vincent agreed that two lyrics, which Bunn had written, be incorporated into the score, that agreement to produce the opera was reached. Strangely enough, they are two of the most popular songs; 'In Happy Moments' and 'Scenes That Are Brightest'. In fairness to Bunn, no effort was spared in the production, and when MARITANA opened on 15 November 1845 its success was unqualified. The leading music critic, J.W. Davison wrote: 'Wallace's MARITANA achieved the most complete success ever witnessed within the walls of an English Theatre'. When he was described as 'the compeer of Balfe' Wallace's future was assured. The music critic of the Illustrated London News wrote: 'When we heard a rehearsal we were fairly taken by surprise; but at once we felt compelled to avow the presence and supremacy of a genius. We predicted a great and decided success by listening only to his inspirations without scenic adjuncts .... and the unknown struggler for musical fame achieved a glorious triumph for himself, for the honour of his country, and for the art which is European'.

A measure of the opera's success is the fact that it was presented for the 50th time as early as 5 February 1846. On this occasion Vincent was accorded a benefit at Covent Garden. As well as the opera, he played his famous composition LA CRACOVIENNE on the piano, vocal pieces were contributed by Miss Rainforth and Signor Marras and violin solos by Mons. Sainton. It was a long night.

Never slow to take advantage, Vincent crossed over to Dublin within a week of this celebration. Sponsored by the Dublin Anacreontic society, he appeared at the historic Rotunda Concert Hall on 9 February to a rousing reception. A concert version of MARITANA was given; Miss Messent and Miss Schloss sang; the famous Irish oboe player Grattan Cooke performed; but the brightest star was the composer with fantasias, rondos, romances and variations on the piano. The packed house could not be satisfied. But for the fact that the Lord Lieutenant was attending in State, and decorum had to be observed, the music might have gone on till dawn.

A return visit was inevitable, and the full Drury Lane company came to Dublin for the first full performance in Ireland on 1 July 1846. The Theatre Royal was packed to capacity, despite the great famine then sweeping the country and a real Irish welcome was given to the artists. To which Miss Romer, Mr. Harrison and Signor Borrani responded with enthusiasm, and the night was a triumph. To the delight of Dublin's citizens, or more accurately, those who could afford to buy the tickets, further performances were given on the 4th, 6th and 9th July. All the performers were equally well received.

The spectacular success achieved by Vincent with his first opera MARITANA merits closer examination. The story is simple and appealing; a beautiful young gypsy girl dreams of becoming a Lady at the Royal Court in Madrid, and succeeds in her ambition. In writing the spirited Overture, Vincent is one of the earliest composers to include in it some of the principal songs that feature in the score. Nowadays this is standard practice, but it was comparatively new then. But the success of MARITANA is achieved through its string of lovely tunes; 'The Angels' Chorus', 'The Harp in the Air', 'Alas Those Chimes', 'In Happy Moments', 'Scenes that Are Brightest' and others. Compared to some famous operas, there is an embarrasment of riches there, and even more so if we conisder modern musicals, where a whole show can be built around one hit tune such as 'Don't Cry for Me, Argentina' or 'Bring in the Clowns.'

Many of Vincent's melodies became favourites at the musical evenings that were a feature of English middle-class life before mass entertainment took over. Many a tenor who performed at a social evening would have declaimed 'Yes! Let Me Like a Soldier Fall' in a heroic manner to sustained applause. Even G.B. Shaw admitted that it struck a vein of emotion and feeling among the patriotic listeners. Beale & Co., who had purchased the copyright of MARITANA, would have had broadsheets with every song quickly available and in instrumental arrangements also. Such were the sales of sheet music that the publishers gained undue influence, and it was not unknown for the story line of an English opera to be held up by the insertion of a tuneful ballad that would sell well, however unsuitable it might be for the feeling of the scene.

In addition to his musical success, the stories of his escapades and travels gave Vincent an aura of mystery, and he gloried in his celebrity. His friend Hayward St. Leger, describes meeting him at the theatre one evening: 'He was wearing a white hat with a very broad brim, a complete set of planter's nankeen and he carried a thick stick in his hand.' Vincent never was one to shirk the limelight, so all this adulation came naturally to him. He always had an eye for the ladies, and he soon became the darling of the society soirees.

.It is hardly surprising that an attractive man, with more than a hint of mystery about him, proved irrestible to some ladies who should have known better, and romantic adventures ensued. Vincent is said to have been involved in several duels as a result of these activities, but evidence concerning these 'diversions' is not readily available, as might be expected. This may have been what his son Willy was referring to when he mentioned that his father was an excellent marksman all his life. In the cold light of dawn it must be very comforting when walking to a duel to know that one is the better sharpshooter.

Despite all this activity, Vincent did not neglect other branches of music. He published many pieces for both piano and violin, including Fantasias, romances and sets of Variations. Two in particular, the ballad 'Can'st Thou Forget' and the 'Grande Valse de Concert' were especially in demand. He published arrangements of Irish music, but they were too elegant and florid, as had been previous settings of Irish melodies by Beethoven and others. He was much in demand on the London social scene as a teacher and a performer at fashionable siorees.

Flushed with the success of his two lyrics, which had been inserted into MARITANA, Alfred Bunn wrote a libretto for Wallace, but even he could not overcome its inanities. It has been rightly described by critic H.R. Legge as 'one of the worst librettos in existence'. Matters were not helped when the leading soprano, and star of MARITANA, Miss Romer, became indisposed shortly before the advertised first night, and the eagerly awaited new opera had to be postponed. A new opera by Balfe that was in the course of preparation, THE BONDSMAN, was hurriedly produced instead, and stole Wallace's thunder. On 22 February 1847 MATHILDA OF HUNGARY was finally produced at Drury Lane, and was well received. The critic's thought it musically a distinct improvement on MARITANA, but the public did not support it. Since it was based on a European folk legend, Wallace was invited to Vienna to produce it there. This time it was more successful, running for three weeks. The King of Belgium, then on a visit, was particularly enamoured of it, and Wallace cleverly dedicated it to him; apart from gaining the King's friendship, he also gained a valuable gold ring.

THEATRE ROYAL, DRURY LANE.

. *To prevent any further disappointment to the Public and to do full justice to Mr. WALLACE's OPERA, its First Performance is deferred until* **Monday next,** *to allow ample time for Miss ROMER's recovery from her late sudden indisposition—and all Tickets issued for To-night, will be admitted on Monday, until which Evening there will be no Performance.*

*** FIRST NIGHT OF THE NEW OPERA!
AND
NINTH NIGHT OF THE NEW BALLET OF ACTION,
IN WHICH
MADEMOISELLE
MARIETTA BADERNA,
(Principal Dancer from La Scala and other chief Theatres in Italy) and
MONSIEUR CROCE
(From the same Theatre) **WILL HAVE THE HONOR OF APPEARING.**

On MONDAY, NEXT, February 22nd, 1847,
Her Majesty's Servants will perform (*FOR THE FIRST TIME*) a New

GRAND OPERA, in Three Acts,
ENTITLED
MATILDA
OF HUNGARY!

THE MUSIC COMPOSED EXPRESSLY FOR THIS THEATRE BY W. V. WALLACE,
WHO WILL, ON THIS OCCASION, PRESIDE IN THE ORCHESTRA.

The Band, which has been considerably augmented, will be led by Mr. R. HUGHES.
The Chorus, materially increased, under the direction of Mr. TULLY.

Owing to the necessity of **ENLARGING** *the Orchestra, several Subscribers have obligingly consented to the removal of their Stalls.*

THE NEW & EXTENSIVE SCENERY BY MR. GRIEVE, MR. TELBIN, & ASSISTANTS.
The Properties and Decorations by Mr. BLAMIRE.
The Costumes by Mr. BOVEY, Mrs. BALLS, and Assistants,   The Machinery by Mr. B. SLOMAN.
THE INCIDENTAL DANCES ARRANGED BY MONSIEUR ADRIEN.

The whole produced under the superintendance of Mr. W. WEST.

Count Magnus, *(First Minister of Bohemia)* Mr. BORRANI,
Prince Ottokar,   *(Chief Secretary)*   Mr. S. JONES,
          Count Ituriz, *(Commander of the Forces)* Mr. SIMMONDS,
Count Oxfern, Mr. HOWELL,   Vladimir, *(a Senator)* Mr. BURT,
George Podiebrad,   -   Mr. W. HARRISON,
     Mathias,   *(an Innkeeper)*   Mr. WEISS,
Attendant,   Mr. HEATH,   Officer,   Mr. MORGAN,

43

Before returning to London plans had been made for a production of MARITANA in the new year.

When he had rapidly departed from Sydney nine years previously Vincent's sister, Eliza remained there. A soprano herself, she later married John Bouchelle, also a singer, but was widowed while still young. In 1847 she arrived in London, and at the end of the year she travelled with Vincent to Vienna where MARITANA was to be produced. It was staged on 8 January 1848 at the Theatre auf der Wieden,

MATILDA Colour Picture

and turned out to be one of his greatest triumphs. The magnificent singing of leading soprano Standigl helped Maritana on her triumphal way, and was in itself a compliment to the composer. It was repeated on 10 January and again on 17 January, when Vincent was given several curtain calls from the Viennese, who appreciated and loved he melodic flow of his music. The opera ran until the end of February, which itself was no mean achievement; it was a unique feat in view of the repertory system in vogue in opera houses at that time. Not until Mascagni's opera CAVALLERIA RUSTICANA in 1891 swept everyone off their feet would Vienna welcome a foreign composer with such hysterical abandon.

But it was not all sunshine and bouquets. Still awaiting his first opera production in Vienna, Wagner was not amused at the success of a foreigner. Neither was Lortzing, then the most popular of living German composers who described Vincent disgruntedly as: 'That Englishman who has conquered the hearts of the Viennese'. Writing to his friend J.W. Davison, music critic of The Times, Vincent said: 'Some of the papers have commenced a crusade against English art and artists; first Hatton, then Balfe, who is unmercifully torn. My turn comes next. I am accused of not being English enough. They say I am at one moment German, at another Italian, anything but British. Now I am at a loss when I am spoken to about an English Opera School, never having heard of such a thing'.

On their return to London Eliza made her debut at a concert given by the Sacred Harmonic Society in Haydn's CREATION. She must have made a good impression, for on 9 October 1848 she made her Covent Garden debut in, what else, but MARITANA. The critic of the 'Morning Post' liked her performance: 'She is a soprano of good quality and ample range; her execution is facile, and her divisions were managed clearly; but her performance lacked brilliance and spontaneity. She acted with considerable self possession, but lacks grace of action and movement'. It was a different story in 'The Illustrated London News'; 'After making allowances for her nervousness on her debut, it must be said that the attempt was a mistake. There is a notable difference between singing in a concert room and singing on the stage. It is inconceivable that she was thought to possess the qualities of a Prima Donna'. Eliza's name does not crop up again until Vincent used his influence to get her work as a concert singer touring with the pianist Moreau Gottschalk around America.

Hector Berlioz first came to London to conduct opera during the season by Julien at Covent Garden in 1848. He returned in 1851 during the Great Exhibition promoted by Prince Albert at Alexandra Palace, and in 1852 and 1855 to conduct the National Philharmonic Orchestra. During 1853 he had the honour of conducting his own opera BEN-VENUTO CELLINI at Covent Garden. He met Vincent and they became close friends. Berlioz had happy memories of those times, as he related in his autobiography: 'We spent many evenings together in London around a bowl of punch, as he told me of his strange adventures, and I listened avidly. He has taken women, and he has fought several duels, unhappily for his opponents. He is a fine eccentric man, outwardly calm like certain Englishmen, yet basically reckless and aggressive like an American."

At that time Vincent had started to write his third opera, to a libretto by Fitzball, based on the legend of the Lorelei. Thus Vincent anticipated Wagner; firstly by using the story of the Lorelei; secondly by setting one of the scenes in an underwater cave in the Rhine. In August 1848 Vincent received a commission from the Paris Opera House to compose an opera, a fact confirmed by both Grattan Flood and Pougin. The grandiose settings and story of LURLINE would have been eminently suitable for spectacular production in the Parisian style. But fate intervened. Vincent's eyesight deteriorated, and he had to put away the unfinished score. In a sad letter to Anna Jones (nee Kelly), his sister-in-law, Vincent later wrote:
'After all I had suffered, and just at the moment that I had hoped by one bound to gain an illustrious reputation by producing an opera in Paris, imagine my feelings, being almost blind, and without a hope of being able to do anything for a year or two'.
Had he been able to fulfil that contract, and with a genuinely dramatic libretto to build on, Vincent could well have written the great opera that elude him. Instead he retired to the Channel Islands to recover in cosseted luxury. The completing of LURLINE would have to wait for more than a decade of change and maturing in Vincent's music. Yet strangely a version of the opera, called LORELY, was produced in Germany in 1854.

LURLINE 'Quadrille'

CHAPTER SIX

– Wandering Again –

Vincent then travelled extensively as conductor of a concert party through South and Central America. He renewed old friendships, revisited the scenes of past triumphs, and conquered new audiences. It has been unkindly said of him: 'he came, he saw, he conquered; but never did he stay long enough in any one place'. But he brought good music and talented musicians to many culturally starved people in Brazil, Chile and Peru; travelling to many isolated towns that European musicians did not want to hear about, much less go to the danger and trouble of visiting. It was a very successful and financially rewarding tour, as well as giving Vincent inspiration and time to assimilate and store away new ideas and idioms.

An article in the magazine 'The Message Bird' of New York, dated 1st July 1850, seems to be the result of an interview with Vincent.

'William Vincent Wallace has returned to the United States after an absence of seven years, which he has passed in placing himself permanently upon the list of musicians whose fame entitles them to be known in after times. He is now in New York, though he is leaving shortly and spending the summer season at one of the lakes to resume composing'...

He has now been absent from London some seven or eight months, during which he has been in South America. While at Rio de Janerio he played before the Emperor and Empress of Brazil; the former of whom, is a 'fanatico' in music. He was so delighted with the superb talents of Wallace on the piano that he expressed his feelings in an unimperial manner; he expressed himself with the energy and fervour of a citizen of the world; in admiration of the genius who had delighted him with his inspirations the Emperor pressed upon his acceptance a valuable diamond ring which Wallace of course accepted'.

On his approach to St. Louis Wallace met with one of those Providential escapes which seem to be granted to men of his talent alone. He was a passenger on the ill-fated steamer St. Louis when it's boiler exploded, causing death and injury to over fifty people. A few minutes before the explosion Wallace was on deck, within a few feet of the boilers, when he was sent for by the ladies in the cabin to redeem a promise he had made to play some music for them. He was seated at the piano, and had hardly struck the keys but few times before his was answered by the ordnance of death below. For an instant they thought he had shattered the piano, and confusion and dismay overcame the company so lately composed by the charm of his music ... The wails of the dying, and the frantic shrieks of the wounded and the scalded, as they writhed in agony on the deck below, or leaped in madness into the turbid river, told the tale of horror. It brought a finale to his brief overture more fearful than any composer, in his maddest moments of inspiration, ever dreamed of. That frightful night and the next painful morning, as the sufferers groaned and died around him, will never be forgotten by Wallace'....

'After the production of his operas MARITANA and MATILDA OF HUNGARY in London, he went to Vienna where MARITANA scored another triumph. He then composed LURELEIGH, to a book of Fitzball's ; a singular coincidence, as the last work on which the lamented Mendlssohn was engaged was also LORETZ, the book of that fine poet Gerbel. This is an exquisite opera, and the book is in the hands of Mr. Beale. It will probably be produced by him in Berlin during the ensuing winter (1850/51), under the management of the celebrated Meyerbeer, who is a personal friend of Wallace. He has also written the opera GULNARE for Milan; another named OLGA to a book of Count Peopli, the author of PURITANI; and a third called THE MAID OF ZURICH, to a book by Fitzball, which is to be produced by the English Opera this season. When Wallace played over the airs of LURLEIGH to Jenny Lind, she promised him that, if she had the opportunity, she would sing in the opera.

'From these details it will be seen that Wallace is a hard and resolute worker. When it is remembered that he is not yet thirty-six years of age, it will be granted that he has done more than any living composer towards securing for himself a deathless reputation. As compared with Balfe, who entered the race for reputation long before him, we have little hesitation in placing Wallace at the head of the writers of English opera. Especially when it is remembered that his approach to the theatre only began six years ago. At present Wallace shares the throne of English music with Balfe; it will not be long before he outstrips his fellow Irishman.'

In these days those with artistic talent, to a greater or lesser degree, employ costly managers and agents to ensure their names remain before the public; judging by that article Vincent managed it nicely on his own. It would be interesting to know who coined the description 'International Celebrity Artist': because once again this description fitted Vincent like a glove. American music lovers were unlikely to have forgotten such an outgoing performer as he was, but just in case, he hit the headlines again.

In London he had met a young pianist of German descent, Helen Stoepel, when she accompanied Eliza at a concert. In June 1850 Helen made her debut in New York at the Tabernacle. Together with her family, she was connected with the Moravarian Singers and the Germania Quartet. Her brother, Franz, appeared in concerts with Eliza, while another brother, Robert, composed a number of operas that were staged in America. When they had first met, Vincent and Helen had not taken much notice of each other; this time they took a lot of notice. In October 1850 Vincent married Helen, despite having a wife and son in England. Later he explained to his favourite sister-in-law, Anna, that he felt that his marriage to Alica had never been legal because of the pressure on him to change his religion and because he was too young to properly understand the obligations it entailed.

How he convinced the authorities of his freedom to marry Helen is not clear. Perhaps it was to give some semblance of legality to the marriage that he took out American citizenship shortly afterwards; at least it would be legal according to their laws. The couple certainly were an attraction when appearing on the concert platform as 'Mr. and Mrs. Wallace - Piano and Violin Duettists'. Though she was much younger than he, they were very happy, and had tow sons, Clarence (1852) and Vincent (1854). Helen survived Vincent by thirty years, teaching music in Broklyn to eke out a precarious living. As early as 1854 Vincent suffered the first of his many heart attacks, and his ophthalmia flared up again, as did rheumatism in his hands. If only Hollywood or Televsion had arrived much sooner Vincent would have been made, as his life story is the stuff of which soap operas, if not musical operas, are made. And what a difference it would have made to Vincent's finances, his life, and possibly his health and longevity.

We see Vincent in a new guise in this extract from Moreau

Gottschalk's lifestory. Now 25 years old, he has spent years studying and making a name for himself in France and on the Continent, and has arrived in New York to begin his professional career in America.

In his letters to his father written after his departure from Spain he had insisted that the man of all men to manage his American debut was William Vincent Wallace, in New York since 1851 in company with his new wife, a professional pianist, and his sister, an opera and concert soprano. Gottschalk has also addressed several appeals direct to Wallace, but had left Europe too soon to receive answers. Now, in a hansom cab with his father and brother driving to the Irving House, he learned that the Irishman, touched over the trust placed in him, had made all arrangements for the debut.

"There were to be two concerts. While the first, to come on Friday 11 February 1853, would be small and intimate, the second, announced for the following Thursday, was to be in all respects grand. The man employed by Wallace to direct the publicity had already proved himself an expert advertiser, and the current issue of Graham's Magazine carried a long biographical article on Gottschalk, as did other pamphlets in New York bookstores."

"Gottschalk had scarcely settled with his father and brothers in a suite at the Irving House when Wallace called. There was an hour of jolly talk. Then the Irish manager presented Gottschalk with a list of the private homes in which he was to play in the course of the next three weeks. In these salon appearances, as well as on the occasion of a recital at Irving House for representatives of the Press, Gottschalk avoided the music announced for his concerts, and confined himself mainly to Spanish dances culled from 'El Sitio de Zaragoza', Chopin mazurkas and waltzes, and several new compositions by Wallace."

"In the year 1853 only three pianists with European reputations comparable to Gottschalk's had played in New York, and the debut of each was either flat or vulgar ... Wallace had planned to make Gottschalk's debut novel, dignified and persuasive. He showed that he was a manager with foresight."

"The first of the two concerts, on Friday 11th February, was in every way modest. the place was Niblo's Saloon, a concert hall adjacent to the great theatre used mainly for opera, Niblo's Garden. Wallace had fixed the hour at seven-thirty so that patrons could, if they liked, leave immediately after the conclusion of the concert, pass down a corridor, and reach their seats in the theatre in time to hear Madame Sontag in her first big aria in LA SONNAMBULA. If Gottschalk that evening missed the elegance of the aristocrats who thronged to his concerts in Paris, he at least found the flowers and the perfume. He also found every seat in the hall occupied."

"The programme required little more than an hour. Appearing with Gottschalk were piano-duettist Richard Hoffman and soprano Rosa de Vries, the one woman singer in New York that season able to hold public favour in competing with Mesdames Sontag and Alboni. The audience applauded warmly; Gottschalk even heard the first time in a concert, whistling. Never before had he played 'Le Bananier' in public without being required to repeat it; he felt that his hearers wanted to express their appreciation with the enthusiasm of Europeans, but for some reason they did not dare."

"Though the reviews the next day were all highly favourable, Gottschalk was not sure about the success of his first appearance until the next Thursday evening, when he faced his second New York audience. This time his hearers were numbered by the thousand. 'A mere pianist' the Times reported the next morning 'had filled the great Niblo's Garden from pit to ceiling'."

"Wallace chose a night when there was no performance of opera, and engaged the full orchestra, he himself serving as conductor. Gottschalk was to say later that in his first number, Weber's 'Concertstuck', he had never had more sympathetic orchestral support. Again Mr. Hoffman appeared at the second piano, while Madame de Vries sang, as did basso Luigi Rocco, another singer much liked in New York. It seemed to Gottschalk this time that the New Yorkers had come out of their shells. 'The flattering demonstration of favour', as one newspaper called the applause, made him feel that Americans were almost as receptive as Spaniards. he had to repeat both 'Bamboula' and 'Le Bananier'."

"The critics agreed that the two concerts constituting the American debut were a great triumph for the Louisianan, and all emphasised his virtuosity. In writing of his work as a composer, most of them chose the 'Jerusalem' Fantasy and 'The Carnival of Venice' for extended praise. Not one of them pointed out anything of special interest to Americans in the original music. They wrote of Gottschalk as they might have written of Liszt, Thalberg or Prudent."

In planning the two concerts Wallace gave little thought to expense. On the final reckoning, Gottschalk discovered that his American debut had cost him $2,400. While the bills were still coming in, P.T. Barnum offered him $20,000 a year to clear off all expenses for a two or three year tour of the United States. The young man was tempted to accept, but refused on his father's advice. He began the first of his many American tours instead, and featured some Wallace compositions on his programmes. Vincent's sister, Madame Bushelle, travelled as a singer with the touring party.

As ever with Vincent, the far away fields seemed greener, and this time the travel bug took him back to London early in 1854. But not for long as he embarked on a Continental concert tour. This came to an abrupt end as Europe was now dangerous territory because of wars and rumours of wars. So that on the 28th of September 1854 Vincent was on board the ship 'Arabia' bound for America again. He had barely landed when he was on the podium conducting MARITANA in New York on the 19th of October. The Pyne Harrison Company were also in New York at the Broadway Theatre, and they presented THE BOHEMIAN GIRL and MARITANA there with Vincent conducting. Before the end of the year the Pyne Harrison Company gave Vincent a benefit night at which MARITANA was again performed.

At a concert given by the Eisfeld Quartette in Dodsworth's Hall, New York on the 26th January 1856 the solo pianist was Helen Stoepel. In spite of her own standing as a concert pianist, she was listed as Mrs. William Vincent Wallace. Presumably the name of Wallace, either as a composer, or as a musician, or as a man with a tinge of scandal about him, had greater drawing power than that of Stoepel, though that family were well known as musicians, especially among the large German community.

CHAPTER SEVEN

– *Back in London* –

But Wallace soon tired of the 'life in a goldfish bowl' that celebrity becomes in America, and once again came back to London. He resumed his teaching activities, his salon appearances and his composition. His ballads were very popular at this time; one 'Why do I weep for thee' being a favourite of Irish born soprano Catherine Hayes (who was buried near him in Kensal Green Cemetery): another 'The Bell Ringer' was a perennial part of Charles Stanley's concert programmes. As early

Wallace c. 1860

as 1848 Wallace had produced a Fantasia based on LUCRETIA BOR-
GIA by Donizetti. But music moves on, and the Fantasia he wrote in
1859 was based on RIENZI by Wagner, followed interestingly in 1860
by Beethoven's THE RUIN OF ATHENS. He also turned his hand to
Irish music, wiring an arrangement of 'Garryowen', 'The Coolun' and
'St. Patrick's Day' in 1859. As well as transcriptions, he also wrote a
good deal of original work for the piano and the violin. France and
Germany also claimed his attention in 1858, and he travelled widely as a
conductor and soloist.

'During the whole of the nineteenth century continual efforts
were made to establish some kind of National Opera House' states E.W.
White. 'For a short period the Lyceum Theatre functioned as The
English Opera House; but after Balfe's scheme of 1841 collapsed, it abandoned any consistent operatic policy. It would be true to say that for the
earlier part of the nineteenth century Drury Lane was virtually the home
of English opera. Under the successive managements of Arnold, Elliston
and Bunn it became the centre for the operatic productions of Bishop,
Balfe, Benedict and Wallace .... Even so it must be remembered that
these operatic performances were never given in the form of a continuous season, but were interpolated between the plays that were the vehi-
cle for Drury Lane's star actors such as Edmond Kean (who was born a
year before Wallace in the same house in Waterford) and William
Charles Macready'.

As E.W. White continues the story in 'The Rise of English
Opera':
'About ten years later Balfe was associated with another English
National Opera scheme. This time the initiative came from two singers,
Miss Louisa Pyne and Mr. William Harrison, who entered into a part-
nership and organised a company for the performance of opera in
English. They started at the Lyceum Theatre, then moved to Drury lane,
and were finally promoted to Covent Garden, where they gave regular
seasons during the autumn and winter from 1857 to 1864. In the course
of their comparatively brief existence they presented translations of various Italian and French operas (including some by Auber), and no less
than fifteen new English operas, of which six were by Balfe, and three by
Wallace'.

In 1859 the Pyne Harrison Company became lessees of the
Covent Garden, and among the successes of their first season there were

Thursday, Friday, & Saturday,

FEBRUARY 23rd, 24th, and 25th, 1860

WILL BE PRODUCED,

With New Scenery by Messrs. T. GRIEVE and TELBIN.

The Costumes by Mr. JAMES and Mr. COOMBES,   The Properties by Mr. PRESCOTT

Machinery by H. SLOMAN,   The Dances arranged by Mons. PETIT

And the Opera produced by Mr. EDWARD STIRLING.

AN OPERA, ENTITLED

LURLINE

THE MUSIC

By W. VINCENT WALLACE,

THE LIBRETTO BY E. FITZBALL.

Count Rudolph,	(a Young Nobleman)	Mr. W. HARRISON,
Wilhelm,	(his Friend)	Mr. LYALL,
Rhineberg,	(the River King)	Mr. SANTLEY,
The Baron Truenfels,	-	Mr. G. HONEY,
Zelieck,	(a Gnome)	Mr. H. CORRI,
Adolph, Mr. MENGIS,	Conrade, Mr. FRIEND,	
Ghiva,	(the Baron's Daughter)	Miss PILLING,
Liba,	(a Spirit of the Rhine)	Miss FANNY CRUISE,
	AND	
Lurline,	(Nymph of the Lurlie Berg)	Miss LOUISA PYNE.

Vassals of Rudolph,   Attendants of Baron,   Conspirators,
Pages,   Water Spirits, &c., &c.

Conductor,   Mr. ALFRED MELLON.

LURLINE Poster

56

Balfe's ROSE OF CASTILLE and SANTANELLA, and Wallace's MARITANA. Naturally enough they approached Vincent to compose a new opera for the following season. Resourceful as ever, Vincent took down a dust-covered score from the shelf on which it had reposed patiently for the past decade. Now a widely travelled musician, and well aware of current musical trends, he re-wrote the score with a considerable change of style. Thus more than ten years later, and at Covent Garden instead of the Paris Opera, LURLINE saw the light of day on the 23rd February 1860. Bunn is also said to have intended producing it in 1948 at Drury Lane, but he encountered one of the financial crises that seemed to bedevil opera houses, and that dream faded.

Described as a 'Grand legendary opera in 3 Acts' LURLINE proved an unqualified success, and ran to the end of the season, being performed twentythree times. Generally considered to be Vincent's best and most ambitious work, it was acclaimed as the musical event of the season. In Grove VI, N. Temperly wrote: 'The drinking chorus 'Drain the cup of pleasure' has the force of a Verdian chorus; the trio 'Ah dare I hope' has as much action and characterisation as the entire opera of Balfe's. Even the critic Cornetto de Bassetto grudgingly admitted that 'if Wallace's inspiration had been a trifle more sustained, LURLINE might well have taken its place at the head of all English operas.'

A large part of the blame of this not happening must be laid at the feet of the incompetent librettist Fitzball, who watered down the legend, and contrived to achieve a happy ending. Unfortunately Vincent failed to treat the mystical theme with the intense conviction it required, and allowed himself to be side-tracked by Fitzball's now dated romanticism. Music critic J.W. Klein wrote in 'Wallace - A Reacessement': 'In LURLINE Wallace believed he had at last surpassed his rival Balfe; many indeed shared his view, and proclaimed it openly'. It was Vincent who was' the English Meyerbeer', while Balfe was scornfully dismissed as the equivalent of the nondescript and fairly frivolous Auber.

As ever with Vincent, there is another side to the story. For some unfathomable reason he sold the performing rights of LURLINE to the Pyne Harrison Company for the sum of ten shillings. The deed of assent of sale can be seen in the British Museum. He then gave the money to the widow of the recently deceased stage carpenter at Covent Garden. So all his labours were for nothing, while the Pyne Harrison Company are reputed to have made Fifty Thousand pounds from the

LURLINE Scene

opera. Is it any wonder that on the occasion of the Golden Jubilee cele-
brations of MARITANA in 1995 Vincent's son wrote to the English
papers complaining that:
'It is cruel that, while much money should still be made out of MARI-
TANA, that the wife and son of the composer should be in dire want'.
It is not recorded if the British public, claimed to be the most generous in
the world, proved that statement correct by helping them. The son,
William, finished his days, sadly, as a poor brother in the Charterhouse.

LURLINE is the only one of Vincent's operas which Arthur
Pougin, the leading music critic in Paris, submits to a searching analysis
in his critical biography of Vincent. After first suggesting that the subject is banal and trite he comments: 'the work is lacking neither in
grandeur nor grace, neither charm or poetry'. He describes the Overture
as 'heroic', with influences of Weber's OBERON, and says: 'it is moulded with uncommon cleverness, orchestrated with pomp, and splendidly
constructed'. But he felt LURLINE was no masterpiece because of a
lack of unity.
'In this respect the work offends. The score lacks a 'colour sui generis,' a
personal style - intentional, energetic, so exact at depicting the senti-

ments which it expresses so exactly ... LURLINE is a remarkable, if incomplete work, elegant to a supreme degree, quite appropriate to the exigencies of the scene. But the style is composite.'

Pugin explains the last sentence by pointing out that Vincent was familiar with the music of the leading opera composers of his time from Auber through Bellini, Donizetti, Herold and Meyerbeer to the great Rossini. It may be assumed that at some stage he had also heard works by Verdi and Wagner. When Wagner was first heard in England in the 1850's the listeners were shocked at his revolutionary methods; one critic described a Wagnerian composition as 'a wild and extravagant piece of demagogic cacophony'. As any open minded composer should, Vincent made himself aware of current musical ideas and trends, and imperceptably changed his own train of musical thought. This hardly justifies Pougin's charge that Vincent's music was composite and derivative. The great musicologist Dr. Burney is worth quoting on this point:
'The scale, harmony and cadence of the music being settled, it is almost impossible for any composer to invent a genus of composition that is wholly and rigorously new, any more than for a poet to form a language-idiom and phraseology for himself. All that the greatest and boldest musical inventor can do is to avail himself of the best effusions, combinations and effects of his predecessors, to apply and arrange them in a new manner, and to add from his own personal source whatever he can draw that is grand, graceful, gay, pathetic or in any other way pleasing.'
Who would like to say that Vincent either failed or neglected his art, as seen by Dr. Burney? Every composer in his early works naturally gives hints of what previous composers influenced his studies and feelings for music; the luckier ones develop a style of their own that masks these derivations, but not all are so highly gifted, or so lucky.

One of the puzzling aspects about Vincent's output of music is the difference of opinion about how many operas he wrote, and the order in which they were composed. The first two, MARITANA (1845) and MATILDA OF HUNGARY (1847) are fully documented. He is said to have completed LURLINE in July 1848, and Bunn was to have presented it at Covent Garden during the winter season. In his autobiography written in 1859, Fitzball states:
"I have written two works for Vincent Wallace, already purchased, which I anxiously wish to see produced; they are splendid efforts of fine musical conception and composition. I predict for them a great career"

One of these must have been LURLINE, but what of the other? In the interview with Vincent given in the 'Message Bird' of New York in July 1850, an opera called "THE MAID OF ZURICH, from a Book by Fitzball, is to be produced by the English Opera this season". This would appear to be the second libretto mentioned by Fitzball. So THE MAID OF ZURICH would appear to have been Vincent's fourth opera.

Yet it has been claimed that after LURLINE was completed Vincent was commissioned to write an opera to a libretto by Joseph Edward Carpenter. He went so far as to sketch out the music for THE KING'S PAGE, but nothing is known of it since. In the same 'Message Bird' interview of 1850 it is stated: "he has also written the opera GULNARE for Milan, and another named OLGA". This is very puzzling, as Vincent is believed to have written these two operas while in Weisbaden in 1858/59; yet here they are mentioned in an article dated 1st July 1850.

The circumstances of Vincent's next venture into opera are explained by J.W. Klein:
"A strange and highly significant change was gradually coming over the gay and carefree creator of MARITANA. Fitzball's mechanical and mawkish rhymes were beginning to nauseate him; he hankered after something more austere and even exalted. Accordingly he entrusted the eminent critic H.F. Chorley with the book of his next opera. The result was Wallace's most readable and plausible libretto; occasionally this grim story of the innocent girl malevolently accused of witchcraft seems to look forward to the magnificent play "The Crucible" by Arthur Miller. Wallace made a serious attempt to infuse the hitherto missing element of stark drama into his opera, which is characterised by a greater continuity of texture than his previous works ... Above all the trial scene in the third act is gripping; for a moment the light-hearted Wallace succeeds in creating an atmosphere of grave solemnity. Exultantly he declared 'This is my finest opera'. Yet one disastrous weakness ruined everything; the final act is a dreadful anti-climax. How amazing that a critic with such a high artistic standard as Chorley should have stooped, at so crucial a moment, to the level of a Bunn or a Fitzball. To end an essentially tragic opera with the merriest of merry rondos was bound to rob the work of all consistency. A little more daring on the part of both librettist and composer might have ensured a lasting success for THE AMBER WITCH".

It was first produced at His Majesty's Theatre on the 28th of February 1861, and according to The Times critic: "The house was enthusiastic in demonstration of approval, the applause was incessant, and many pieces were re-demanded. the singers, in emulation of the example recently set by Simms Reeves, invariable and respectfully declined the honour .... The principal singers were recalled after every act, and at the conclusion of the opera, similar compliments were paid to Mr. Charles Halle, the conductor, who thoroughly deserved it.". Like every story about the composer, there is a twist in it. Shortly after THE AMBER WITCH opened, one of the financial crises endemic to English opera managements took place, forcing the closure of His Majesty's Theatre. When passing the closed Theatre one Sunday afternoon, Mapleson, the current lessee of Covent Garden ,saw the costumes for THE AMBER WITCH on stands outside the Theatre. He promptly borrowed them, re-engaged the cast, and staged the opera at Covent Garden. Sadly his brilliant opportunism was not rewarded, as the public did not take the opera to its heart, feeling that the whole thing was not English enough. So much for English opera, and the future of English opera composers.

LOVE'S TRIUMPH

Not easily daunted, Wallace set to work on his next opera. This time he turned to the distinguished veteran writer, J.R. Planche, whose libretto is worthy in every way of its accomplished author. It is based on the comedy 'Le Portrait Vivant' produced at the Theatre Francaise some years previously. In LOVE'S TRIUMPH there is a great deal of French style; in composing it Wallace had visions of the Opera Comique in Paris. It is light, gay and sparkling, and is strongly reminiscent of the French composer Auber. With a well-crafted libretto, and a score of masterly clarity to carry the story along, LOVE'S TRIUMPH had a long run ahead of it. The librettist, Planche, explains graphically what happened. The first performance was on the 3rd of November 1863. 'Being produced before Christmas, as soon as the holiday arrived it was sacrificed, as too many have been before it, to the pantomime ... Several airs were omitted, duets and concerted pieces cruelly hacked and mutilated without reference to the author or the composer'.

In spite of this debacle, Wallace had another opera ready for the Pyne Harrison Company next year. In fact the season was opened with the first production on the 12th of October 1863 of THE DESERT FLOWER. This was an English version by librettists A. Harris and J. Williams of the opera JAGUARITA D'INDIENNE by the French composer Halevy, which had been successful with soprano Marie Cabel starring. The Times critic reported: 'The opera, splendidly got up and admirably performed, was received by the densely crowded audience with warmest applause. The crowded house had an air of brilliancy of fashion seldom seen at this season of the year. The Royal box was occupied by members of the Royal Family of Denmark, now visiting England.... It is another instance of the injury done to the musical stage by want of attention paid to the dramatic character of pieces brought upon it. Our composers accept anything in the shape of a libretto that is put in their hands: we constantly find composers of genius and reputation throwing away really fine music upon namby-pamby and nonsense'.

'Based on Cooper's book 'Tales of American Life', the desert flower of the title is the chieftainess of a tribe of American Indian warriors at odds with the inhabitants of a white man's settlement. Their military commander meets, and falls in love with her, to their mutual surprise; (but not ours, given reasonable familiarity with opera plots) ... Such being the dramatic quality of the opera, it is easy to see that its success must mainly depend upon its music. Wallace's reputation is well established, and will be maintained by the music of THE DESERT FLOWER. It has all the freshness, vigour, grace and melody which abound in all of Wallace's works; and it is written with even more than his usual correctness and purity of style'. But the knowledgeable critic seems to have been sadly mistaken, or else the public was, for they stayed away and doomed the opera. It was replaced by a new work by Balfe, BLANCHE DE NEVERS, based on the popular drama 'The Duke's Motto'. This was also dismissed as not being English enough, as was Wallace's; Balfe's opera was no more successful than Wallace's, which had been replace with indecent and unfortunate haste.

This was the last of Wallace's operas to reach the stage. He did not give up, and had started work on another opera. According to Willim Spark it was called THE MAID OF ZURICH, but Grattan Flood in his 'Memoir' says it was called ESTRELLE. The entry in Grove V says: 'that after his death Wallace's wife gave the unfinished opera ESTRELLE to W.K. Bassford to complete'. Wouldn't it be interesting to discover the whereabouts of that score. Either way Wallace's ill-health intervened, and he laid the work aside.

CHAPTER EIGHT

– *The Last Act* –

Because Vincent had spent so much time chasing around the world, and had no real home anywhere, (even in London he lived at several different addresses), practically nothing in the way of documents or letters has survived. In his biography of Wallace, Perceval Graves quotes from two; one to his son William, and one to his sister-in-law Mrs. James Jones, formerly Anna Kelly. Here is that letter in full, as it touches on many interesting points.

> 20, Berners Street,
> Oxford Street,
> London.
> 28 Jany. 1859

"My Dear Anna,

Your letter dated 7th Oct. I received from one of the clerks in Cramer and Beale's Music Shop a few days back; another which I found on my table last night bears the date 8th Dec.. Having been in Germany since last September until the 17th Jan., and consequently only a few days in London, you can readily understand why they were not answered.

In the first place I regret most sincerely that your circumstances are so straitened and that your sister should have been so long a burden on you, and I am much surprised that Alicia, whom I understand is without Family, and whose religious sentiments are so profound, should have lost such a good occasion to Prove their sincerity. believe me, when I assure you that I deeply regret that You, above all others should have suffered inconvenience in this Matter, and I take this opportunity of explaining to you why I have not been able to do what my sense of Justice would dictate, even though my recollection of the Past and its useless sacrifices call up feelings of the bitterest kind.

Now, let us go back to the Year 1846 just after I composed

'Maritana'. Travel, Study and Experience had so changed me that I believe you would have with difficulty recognised your companion in the duets of Mayseder at Frescati, but the Heart which you first inspired remained the same, and will ever be so, if its natural impulses are not changed, and any attempt to force me to do that which at present is Perfectly impossible! At the Time I have just alluded to, all things seemed tending to the most brilliant results, and the Studies of years and the total abnegation of very Pleasure for the sake of my Art, were at length to meet a just reward - when, by One horrible Act, Isabella, shattered all her own hopes of happiness, and reduced me to such a nervous state that I was unable to write for nearly three years.

You are not aware perhaps, that by that deed, if it had not been by a kind interposition of Providence, she would have been the cause of my dying a Felon's death, for if I had entered the room alone, a few minutes later, (for nothing but the Maidservants accidental discovery saved her life) the impression would have been that I had committed the dreadful act, and No Power on earth would have saved me from being hanged - ever since this circumstance I have the greatest antipathy to her, it is not hate, God forbid, for I pity her with all my heart, but her presence makes me shudder with horror at the recollection of what has occurred, and I verily believe, that if circumstances ere such that I were obliged to live with her, I should imitate her example, I am led to these remarks by a passage in one of your letters in which you say that you prevented her coming to me. To put an end to this idea at once and for ever, I assure you most solemnly that the day she arrives in London I shall leave England never more to return. I must also state to you, that in the Opinion of some of the First Lawyers in England my connection with Isabella has been from the First, Illegal, as I was bred up a Protestant, and was not at that time 20 Year Old, but for your sake and Willy's I have never thought of raising such a scandalous Question! The best thing after all, is to leave things to take their natural course, and Time will tell whether my intentions are not of the kindest if I am only granted health and strength to work.

For the opinions of others I care little, but I confess that I regard your esteem most highly, for which reason I Place before you the Principal events of my life, so that you may judge for yourself how hard was the Fate which I had to struggle with.

In the year 1848 my health, which had been so bad during the last two years, seemed to take a favourable Turn, and it was during that year that I composed the greater part of the opera LURLINE, but the shock which I had suffered and the almost total want of rest, brought on by an attack of Ophthalmia - Fancy my dear Anna, after all I had suffered and just at the Moment that I hoped by one bound to gain an Illustrious reputation by Producing an Opera in Paris - Imagine my feelings, almost blind, and without a hope of being able to do anything for at least a year or two; upon recovering a little, and finding that I dare not write, I went to South America with the intention of Playing again in Public, but was unable to carry it out from the wretched state of my health, from Rio de Janeiro I went to New York, and there remained for six years, suffering at times most terribly from the repeated attacks which my eyes were subject to whenever I attempted to work more than usual.

At present I am glad to say that I may consider my eyes as quite cured, still, I must not venture to use them at Night. During the last Two Years I have suffered much from Chronic Rheumatism brought on by exposure in the Indies and North America, so bad has it been, that for more than One Year I have been quite unable to play the piano, and it is only within the last Month that I have been able to play at all, the pain that I endure while writing this letter, is almost more than I can bear, and it is only by tying a handkerchief around my hand, that I am enabled to continue at times, it is with the greatest difficulty that I can even sign my Name, Most fortunately for me, the notation of Music does not Produce the same evil effect.

Another source of great discomfort to me is that Willy has grown up most idly inclined, and though I never fail to pay him his allowance of One Guinea a week, he is always in debt, and I am constantly harrassed by his creditors, when I have more troubles of my own than I can bear, however, I had an explanation with him Yesterday and I have told him the position of his Mother and the Necessity of my transferring that allowance over to her, beginning from the 12th February next.

My dear Anna, in the City of London alone, I owe 976 pounds owing to an unsuccessful speculation I made some Years ago in Pianos when I went to South America, and fully Five Hundred Pounds to my American Publisher for Money advanced when I was quite unable to write a Note, I assure you on my word of honour, that I have not gained

Two Hundred Pound a year during the last 5 Years, and out of that I have always paid Willy his allowance. Reputation and Money unfortunately do not go together as you might suppose, and composition is so little profitable that I intend to devote myself to teaching the Piano, but whether I shall do so in London, New York or St. Petersburg (where Balfe had many aristocratic pupils in 1852/3) I have not yet made up my mind, much will depend upon the chances of bringing out an opera here next Autumn. My health is still very bad, and the doctors say that I must return to Wiesbaden in order to be quite cured, but whether I remain here or go to Germany, the allowance shall be paid every month in advance.

But let Isabella remain where she is, or as I said before, her arrival here would be the signal for my instant departure. You may perceive that I write, with great difficulty, it is my intention to go to Ireland next Autumn and then I shall explain to you many things which I do not like to write about. Until then.

Believe me ever Yours

W. Vincent Wallace.

N.B. Pray acknowledge receipt of this letter."

After reading this extraordinary letter, two thoughts immediately spring to mind: firstly, the contrast between the adventurous, exciting, romantic life that Vincent is said to have lived, and the miserable existence described in the letter; secondly, that if Anna Kelly had been down hearted when she wrote to Vincent, she must have felt things were not so bad after hearing from him.

A number of important points do emerge during the course of the letter. All accounts of Vincent's life say that he never saw his wife and son after he left them in Australia. That is clearly not the case. It appears that Vincent and Alicia were living together in London in 1846 when she attempted suicide, and the shock of this caused the final separation. From the letter, and from another to be quoted later, it is obvious that Vincent was in close and regular contact with his son Willy. His ill luck in 1848 when an attack of ophthalmia, probably brought on by overwork on the score, prevented LURLINE being completed for the

Paris opera, deprived him of the opportunity to write the great opera that he, and his contemporaries, felt he had within him.

Vincent claims that his marriage to Alicia is illegal, and then adds: "but for your sake and Willy's I have never thought of raising such a scandalous question". It is entirely understandable that for his son Willy's sake Vincent did not publicly proclaim that the marriage was illegal, thereby making Willy illegitimate. But not raising the scandalous question for Anna's sake ? How or why would the illegality of Vincent and Alicia's marriage affect Anna or reflect badly on her? He rashly states: "but the heart which you first inspired (at Frescati) remained the same, and will ever be so, if its natural impulses are not changed". Bearing in mind that Anna is said to have travelled with them to Australia, and that she and Vincent were good friends at least on the long voyage, perhaps there is another secret here. Could there be other "Wallas" in Australia as well as in New Zealand ?

Great play is made by Vincent of his bad health, and it does sound exaggerated. His companion Wellington Gurney suggested that Vincent's health began to break up round the time THE AMBER WITCH was completed in 1861. He had already suffered heart attacks, and was now diagnosed as having fatty degeneration of the heart, which proved wrong. The treatment for this mis-diagnosis affected his system, and when Vincent left 64 Stratton Street, Piccadilly for Boulogne in 1864 he was never to return. Friends had made available a cottage at Passy near Paris, and there the winter was spent. He was visited daily by Dr. Bouillaud and his son-in-law Dr. Aubursin, who did all in their power to alleviate his sufferings. When asked abut his fees, Dr. Bouillaud insisted: "I am best paid by having saved the life of such an eminent man".

Vincent was still very caught up in his art. The eagerly awaited new production at the Paris Opera was to be the spectacular L'AFRICAINE by Vincent's idol Meyerbeer. A copy of the score was procured, but because of the weight of it, and the weakness of Vincent's hands, he was unable to hold it. Undaunted, he had it cut into manageable sections, examined the work thoroughly, and expressed his appreciation of its merits. It has been said that if L'AFRICAINE could not be ready for production in time, Wallace's LURLINE would be put on in its place. What a fitting farewell to Vincent that would have been, and his dream realised a mere seventeen year late.

But the good doctor was wrong, he had only secured a reprieve.

By April Vincent was well enough to take a short walk nearby, but this led to another attack which confined him to bed permanently. But he was never short of company, among the visitors being Berlioz, Rossini and Thalberg. English friends who visited him included Duggan, Farnie and Osborne. All were shocked at his appearance: instead of the healthy man with brown hair streaked with grey, they now saw him with a thin wan face, his hair now white as snow, and his moustache and beard just as white. Happily his mind never gave away, and he was courteous to the last; in spite of his pain and suffering he was never so petty minded

Wallace c. 1865

as to envy either his contemporaries or his successors.

By September 1865 Dr. Boullaud felt a change of air was needed. A sister of his wife Helen was married to the Marquise de Sante Geme, whose Chateau de Haget in the Haute Pyrenees was made available to him. What more spectacular setting could Vincent have chosen than a Chateau in the clouds in which to spend his final weeks. For sadly that is how it happened.

During all the long months of his final illness Helen was constantly at hand. She anticipated his every wish, and attended his every need. In his turn Vincent was utterly devoted to Helen. It was a great consolation to them to have their two sons with them, Clarence aged 13 and Vincent aged 11; both boys were very musical and later on studied at the Paris Conservatoire. The eldest son of his sister Eliza, J.B. Bushelle, also arrived. Vincent passed peacefully away in the presence of his devoted Helen and family on 12 October 1865.

In reporting Vincent's death, the Revue et Gazette Musicale de Paris commented:
"This man, formerly so vigorous in mind and body, so active, so indefatigable, and who had gone through so many adventures, went to rest calmly: having at his bedside his wife and two sons. His mortal remains are to be taken to England where he will be honoured with a funeral worthy of a great representative".

In London "The Musical Times" reported briefly:
"There was little pomp or ceremony to mark the mournful occasion; but the mute grief of those who pressed around to sob a last farewell as the coffin was lowered, was more eloquent, as a tribute of respect to their brother artist, than all the studied orations that could have been delivered over his grave".

The following report appeared in 'The Orchestra':
"The ceremony took place at 2 o'clock, at which time the weather was much overcast, and though no rain fell, the aspect of the cemetery under the ashen sky and the dripping leaves was melancholy in the extreme ....The chief mourners were his three sons and a nephew. Rivals as well as admirers stood round his grave; composers, singers, critics and publishers. Amongst those present were Sterndale Bennett, Benedict, Macfaren, Sullivan, Planche, Lablanche ... Letters of sympathy were received from Mr. J.V. Davison and Mr. W. Harrison ... It was a tender

and ominous circumstance that as the final words of the funeral service were recited over the composer's tomb, a robin redbreast on a neighbouring branch burst into music, and sang the last and sweetest requiem over the good musician as he was buried"

This incident deeply impressed those present, and inspired Vincent's friend and librettist, H.B. Farnie, to write this touching tribute:

"We stood by the minstrel's grave, silently saying farewell
For we laid him and love his song that long melodious fell;
On the chords of our life he touched, our hearts to his music set,
A music our pleasure and pain will take for their language yet.
But now no tribute of song from quivering lips would come,
And all we had for the master's dirge was a silence too cold and dumb,
Till a wee robin flew to a sprig hanging near,

Wallace's Grave

'Nunc Dimittis' he sang o're the minstrel's bier'.

When Perceval Graves located Vincent's grave in Kensal Green in 1944, he described it as 'a modest white tombstone in the undergrowth'. Earlier this year the undergrowth was very much in evidence, but the tombstone less so. It is now an almost black slab of marble; only with the greatest of difficulty could the name Wallace be read on it. Which is a great pity, because within an arm's length of Vincent's grave is a tall impressive monument to Michael Balfe; to rub it in, there is a fine monument to the British poet Tom Hood within thirty feet in the other direction. Buried close by are the English composers Cooke and Loder, and the great Irish soprano Catherine Hayes, who often sang Vincent's songs.

Letters of Administration of the estate of 'William Vincent Wallace, late of Passy, Paris in the Empire of France, Composer, intestate' were granted to his son and name-sake of '76 Harley Street, Cavendish Square, London, Artist'. The estate was valued at under Eight Hundred Pounds. Willy lived on in genteel penury until his death as a Poor Brother of the Charterhouse on 31 December 1909. His mother, Alicia, returned to Dublin where she taught music, and died in the home of her sister Anna Jones' daughter on 25 July 1900. Vincent's second wife, Helen, spent her latter years as a music teacher in Brooklyn, and died in 1895. Another mystery surrounds the younger sons Clarence and Vincent; both were gifted musicians and attended the Paris Conservatoire; but after being there, there is no account of what happened them.

As Grattan Flood pointed out during the centenary celebrations in Waterford in 1912:
"there is no biography of William Vincent Wallace, no statue or window or memorial slab in Waterford. The greatest of continental cities would have been proud to be recognised as the birthplace of such a composer as Wallace, and gloried in placing a bronze statue in a leading square. Yet there is nothing in Waterford. it has been well said that, like Wren, who built his own memorial in St. Paul's Cathedral, Wallace has bequeathed an enduring memorial of his genius in his operas."

Probably as a result of Grattan Flood's remarks and carried along on the high tide of the centenary celebrations, the saga of the Wallace Plaques began.

Their history dates back to 1912, when there was initiated what was to prove a strangely abortive effort to erect a memorial to a Waterford man whose work will continue for generations to delight all lovers of beautiful melody. On the centenary of Wallace's birth a fund was inaugurated at a representative meeting of Waterford citizens to advance the project which had the two-fold purpose of celebrating the composer's memory and giving a fillip to music in his native city.

The order was entrusted to Mr. W.C. May, the well-known sculptor of the time, who executed the plaques which were to have formed the base of the proposed statue of Wallace. The work was never completed, probably through a lack of finance; and the uncompleted composition became nobody's business, and has lain unhonoured, unnoticed and unwanted in a Waterford store for the past 39 years. Its very existence had, in fact, faded into the background of memory. Worse still, its whereabouts were known to very few until its almost accidental discovery when circumstances necessitated its removal from one store to another.

Then the stone-cut inscription, with the ironic claim 'Erected by his admirers, 1914' protruded through an accumulation of dust. The discovery of these beautiful plaques has, however, served a worthwhile purpose as it has belatedly awakened the interest of those associated with Waterford's present day cultural activities,

The plaques are carved in sections,
and when pieced together read:

WILLIAM VINCENT WALLACE
MUSICIAN AND COMPOSER
Born in Waterford March 11, 1812
Died in Paris, October 12 1865
Buried in Kensal Green, London
MARITANA, LURLINE,
THE AMBER WITCH, etc.

Erected by his Admirers, 1914
William Charles May, Sculptor.

The second plaque bears a realistic stone-cut engraving of the house in Colbeck Street in which Wallace was born. The great tragedi-

an, Charles Kean, was born in the same house a year previously.

The Wallace Plaques were eventually erected, but not on the house in Colbeck Street where Vincent was born. Instead they may be seen just a short walk away on a building that faces up Colbeck Street. The story of how the Plaques arrived at the present situation could have been used as a libretto for a comic opera by Wallace himself. Perhaps we should be happy that at last the beautiful pieces of sculpture are on public display, and do him honour belatedly, in his native city.

CHAPTER NINE

– *Assessment of Wallace* –

Wallace's Achievements:
Before examining Wallace's achievements, it is pertinent to consider the composer's background and character. As the eldest son of an Army bandmaster attached to a British regiment, his educational opportunities would have been very limited. Certainly the musical side of it was capably taken care of, at least as far as his father's knowledge and skill extended. Local teachers were availed of in Waterford and later in Dublin, so a good foundation of musical learning was assimilated. While playing in and leading the orchestra under James Barton, an experienced conductor and teacher, Wallace added invaluable practical experience to the theory of musicianship already filling his head. During the Dublin Music Festival of 1831 the invaluable chance of working closely with Paganini inspired him to try and emulate his hero, and he worked very hard at his violin playing.

Clearly Wallace's musical education was limited. Firstly, because he was busy working and had not the financial means to study full-time. Secondly, because of the limited knowledge and experience of the teachers available to him. Thirdly, because of the limited range of musical activity and audibility in Dublin as compared to London and other European cities. Which prompts the question of how Wallace's talents might have been developed if he had access to the educational and musical opportunities enjoyed, without even thinking of their good fortune, by so many composers considered greater than he.

For reasons of ill-health Wallace went to Australia in 1835, and the British musical scene did not even notice. Over the next ten years he carried the musical flag to many and varied parts of the world, finishing up in America. Whether in concert as a solo pianist or as a solo violinist; playing the music of the masters or his own; when conducting opera or musical performances; all the while he gave untold pleasure to people otherwise denied the joys of hearing good music well performed and presented. The Australians called him 'the Australian Paganini', which surely made him happy. The French colony in New Orleans cheered when the members of the orchestra put down their instruments to applaud 'le jeune Irelandais'. At one concert in Boston he was compared favourably with famous violinists Artot, Ole Bull and Vieuxtemps.

Yet when Wallace arrived in London in 1844 to resume his concert career, he made no impression. It is difficult to believe that his performances could have deteriorated to that extent, given the fact that top European musicians toured regularly in America, and thus long years spent touring and the lack of disciplined practice had caused some diminution in his powers of expression. Or perhaps the English public were too wrapped up in their own performers. Luckily for Wallace, his mind was already set on a new career.

Composition was now his great interest. For the violin he wrote a concerto, a famous set of variations called LA CRACOVIENNE, fantasias, romances and valses. His piano works include three nocturnes, duets, solos and studies. Among the many operas he transcribed are Donizetti's LUCREZIA BORGIE (1848) and Wagner's RIENZI (1859). Two Masses and a cantata, together with many widely sung ballads, cover his vocal work.

Yet Wallace is remembered for composing one or two operas. MARITANA is the monument to his genius, yet LURLINE was almost as successful in its time. 'In 1845 Wallace's MARITANA achieved the most complete success ever witnessed within the walls of an English Theatre' wrote J.W. Davison. Until then Michael Balfe was the undisputed master of the English opera scene, but at one stroke Wallace upstaged him, being hailed as 'the compeer of Balfe'. Together with Balfe's THE BOHEMIAN GIRL, Wallace's MARITANA carried the flag of English opera for the remainder of the century, with Benedict's THE LILY OF KILLARNEY later joining forces to complete the so-called 'Irish Ring' in a sarcastic reference to Wagner's incomparable Ring of the Niebelung. Wallace's opera was rapturously received in Vienna and other cities such as Hamburg, Prague and Wiesbaden. For many years its Overture was very popular on the continent as a concert piece; the French critic Pougin called it 'L'Overture par excellence'.

It is a measure of Wallace's standing in the musical world of his day that the management of the Paris Opera House commissioned an opera from him. The legend of the Lorelei was the chosen subject, a legend well known and well used on the continent, and eminently suitable for a spectacular production in the magnificent splendour of the Paris Opera House. A picture of the flamboyant Wallace triumphantly descending its peerless marble staircase to rapturous applause comes readily to mind. But his dream never happened, for after eagerly working on the score, (perhaps with too much determination), his eyesight failed and he had to put it aside. Ten years later when back in London, he took out the dusty libretto, re-wrote the unfinished score with greater authority and expanded imagination, and the result was LURLINE, an opera that anticipated Wagner in some respects. Even G.B. Shaw, grudgingly confessed 'that if Wallace's inspiration had been more sustained, LURLINE might very well have taken it's place at the head of all English opera'. As a perceptive author and playwright, Shaw should have added that the happy ending tacked on by Fitzball had spoiled the dramatic story, and denied Wallace the powerful emotional situation that would have enabled him to compose the great opera that eluded him. His last three operas, though critically acclaimed, were not successful; they were not English enough, being in the French style of Auber and Offenbach.

Ireland was the birthplace of two of the greatest composers of English opera, Michael Balfe and William Wallace. Strangely enough their work was not influenced by any apparent Irish idiom, nor did either of them make any use in their operas of the great store of Irish songs which several famous continental composers, like Meyerbeer and Flotow, drew upon so eagerly. Perhaps they were both quite confident of their own ability for original composition rather than concern themselves with traditional themes;/or perhaps their upbringing was too far removed from 19th century Gaelic life and culture. It is also likely that their many journeys abroad inevitably moulded their strong cosmopolitan outlook, and that this in turn veered their music away from any native moorings.

Arising from this situation, there are some interesting comments in an article published in 'The Brooklyn Review', dated 13 November 1875:
"The excellence of the ancient music of Ireland is universally acknowledged; of its kind no other country in the world has produced anything to match it in copiousness and beauty. It's range is the widest of any national music, running from the wildest and most rollicksome humour to the gentlest tenderness and the most profound pathos. The men who composed and played this music were confessed masters in their age. The beauty of their compositions and the marvellous skill of their performance excited the hostile Cambrensis to the highest pitch of enthusi-

asm; they were the only things Irish he praised. Orpheus is fabled to have fascinated the wild beasts; Irish ballads really fascinated the brute Cambrensis - a higher achievement - we have his own authority for it.

"Few of our readers are aware of the demands which great modern composers of Europe, 'The Maestri' as they are called, have made on the beautiful relics of our ancient Irish minstrelsy. In the case of some of these appropriations (English and American dramatists who steal their plays from the French call the thievery, most delicately, 'adaptations') the associations are ludicrous. Let us mention one example."

"Mozart was a sincere admirer of Irish music, for he was a great melodist himself, and the relics of our bards are the very soul of melody; so he frequently, and probably unconsciously,worked up snatches from them in immortal compositions. In the 'Gloria in Excelsis' of one of his beautiful Masses he boldly introduces a passage from a notorious Irish bacchanalian song 'The Cruiskeen Laun'. The passage is the refrain that translates as 'We'll quaff the well-filled jug.' This is an instance of the way in which a good reputation will be damaged by vulgar company."

"It is indubitable that this fine air was composed centuries ago, and doubtless for some chant or song of martial triumph. It had the misfortune to be seized on by some drunken rhymer in the last century, who wedded it to the ridiculous words of 'The Crushkeen Laun'. Some of the noblest and most ancient melodies, for the oldest Irish tunes are the best, have suffered sadly in this way. It is the peasantry alone who preserved them; and when the tipsy village bard or the ambitious hedge-school master wanted a tune, he used these to marry to his love-lay or drinking song."

"The old names were thus lost, and the glorious tunes being associated with stupid and vulgar nonsense verse, acquired a certain tone of vulgarity themselves. There is a magnificent Irish melody which the late Dr. Petrie, a great musician and an antiquarian, believed to be one of unknown antiquity. It is know by no other name than as the refrain of a filthy song, written forty or fifty years ago, by some drunken rustic poetaster, who details the results of his foul orgies, how he was jilted, robbed and nearly murdered, adding pathetically 'I'll drink no more on these roads to Sligo'. Milken's preposterous comic song 'The Groves of Blarney' and Father Frank Mahoney's splendid ballad 'The Bells of Shandon' are written to the same old Irish melody - ' The Young

Man's Dream'. Yet the antique tune is degraded by its connection with Milken's vulgar doggerel, while it floats majestically on the tide of Mahoney's full and melodious ballad. It is more familiar these days as 'The Last Rose of Summer''.

"Referring to modern composers, we may mention two out of several instances in which Irish tunes have been appropriated. In operas generally there is one great central tune, from which all the rest of the music branches off, and which gives its peculiar tone and colour to the whole work. In Flotow's graceful opera MARTHA this function is discharged by Moore's lovely melody 'The Young Man's Dream' somewhat clipped and injured by that pedant Stephenson. And 'The Minstrel Boy' acts the same part in Meyerbeer's celebrated opera L'AFRICAINE: perhaps this explains why Wallace liked this opera so much."

"Flotow, who is kapelmeister to the Emperor of Austria, is passionately fond of Irish music, and has made many selections of it for the Imperial band. He never attempted to deny that he made 'The Last Rose of Summer' the substructure of his work; on the contrary, he had an Italian translation of the song itself inserted into the opera."

"It was quite different with the great Jewish Maestro. He never acknowledged what he had done, giving to his act the character of a theft and a fraud. And yet L'AFRICAINE is all 'Minstrel Boy' - it crops up everywhere. To begin with, it runs like a golden thread through the overture. By and by it appears as a single song in all its fullness, and thenceforth we never escape it. The first time we heard the opera, this thing bewildered and worried us greatly. It seemed to us that chorus and orchestra were perpetually on the point of singing or playing the tune over and over again; but after a few bars, suddenly and capriciously changed their minds and turned off into something else."

"In such a manner did Meyerbeer use 'The Minstrel Boy'. Here, was a man, with a vast musical reputation, taking a simple Irish melody, and out of its suggestive and prolific beauty, manufacturing an opera of inordinate length. What a tribute to the musical genius of our Celtic forefathers. Yet Meyerbeer never acknowledged his obligation to Ireland; his love of money was much stronger than his love of truth."

WALLACE'S FAILURES

The first area in which Wallace must be found wanting is in his family life. Having wooed and wed Alicia Kelly, within a couple of years he uprooted her and set off for Australia just when he was making a name for himself. Within a short time of their arrival he left his wife and baby son, leaving them to fend fo themselves while he swanned around the world. He did support them while living in London, but only meagrely so. In support of this is a cutting from a London paper dated November 1895:

"It is curious, as well as painful, to see the coincidence between the fate of the families of two of the most popular British composers. Balfe and Wallace, both Irishmen, write each an opera, THE BOHEMIAN GIRL and MARITANA, that enjoyed, and still enjoys, immense popularity abroad and at home; both had musical fame in paths not common to composers, one as a singer, the other as a violinist; and each, alas, after making much money, left little, and is now represented by a son who has had a hard struggle with poverty. The jubilee anniversary of MARITANA was on 15 November last, and Mr. William Wallace, not unnaturally, has been writing to the papers to suggest that it is cruel that, while much money should still be made out of MARITANA, the wife and son of the composer should be in dire want. No doubt we have moved much since the first night of MARITANA; yet, to the majority of music lovers in England, that simple ballad-opera is still a source of hearty pleasure; and it seems hard to believe that the British public - the most generous in the world - will leave the widow and son of the splendid violinist and popular composer to suffer from poverty in their old age".

This appeal does not seem to have improved matters, as Alicia spent her last years teaching music in Dublin until her death in 1900; William died a poor brother in the Charterhouse in London in 1909. Wallace's fame and fortune did little to improve their lives.

Apart from their financial affairs, Wallace treated his wife and son badly. His claim that she attempted suicide in 1846 may be true, and it may have had a traumatic effect on his sensitive nature, but it begs the question of why she felt driven to this extreme action.   He seems to have never seen her again, and just dumped Alicia on her sisters. He supported his son Willy, but seems to have carefully avoided having much contact with him, so that he drifted impecuniously through his life. In the mid 1850s Wallace arrived back in London with a new wife and two young sons, to which trio he devoted all his attention. This was most uncomplimentary to Alicia and Willy, and very unfair to them.

Whatever talent Wallace had in the musical field certainly did not extend to the business side of his life. After arriving in Sydney he set up the first Music Academy in the Antipodes. Given this and the patronage of the State Governor, Sir Richard Burke, its success should have been assured; but when Wallace disappeared two years later there were debts of Two Thousand pounds outstanding. During his first period in America he invested in a furniture and piano making business. With his high profile as a concert pianist this could hardly go wrong, but it proved to be an expensive failure. Yet amazingly, he was only building up to this greatest debacle.

Wallace abandoned his American career in 1853 and returned to England. But the London musical pool was much bigger than the New York one, and he was not as big a musical fish as he had thought. So he became the darling of the social musical soirees to supplement earnings form teaching and transcribing. In 1858 the libretto of LURLINE inspired him to set about composing his masterpiece. Musically he very nearly succeeded. During what must have been a mental aberration, he sold the copyright to the Pyne Harrison Company for 10 shillings.

Another failing of Wallace's was his inability to judge the librettos offered to him. Bunn's feeble effort for MATHILDA OF HUNGARY has already been castigated. When Fitzball wrote a happy ending to LURLINE instead of the tragic on that the story demanded, Wallace supinely accepted it. In his last opera THE DESERT FLOWER the heroine is the lady chief of an American Indian tribe who falls in love with the military commander who is fighting and killing her people, and Wallace wasted his dwindling energies on such rubbish.

On a musical level, Wallace's free-flowing melodies and vivid orchestration were often too thinly spread. All too often he took the easy way out, and wrote a pretty ballad - even for the villain - when the situation demanded more. The sad thing is that he could write a tragic scene to match and composer when necessary. This was shown in THE AMBER WITCH, which Wallace always claimed to be his best opera. The trial scene in the third act is gripping; he succeeds in creating an atmosphere of grave solemnity. But the final act is a dreadful anti-climax; the work was robbed of all consistency by ending with a rondo. How could the experienced librettist H.F. Chorley destroy the dramatic content? Unfortunately Wallace had not the courage of his own convictions, and failed to insist on the supremacy of his vision. Perhaps he had little choice.

WALLACE'S CONTRIBUTION TO MUSIC

Irish Scene

In all Wallace spent 23 years in Ireland; 15 growing up mostly in Waterford, and 8 as a young musician in Dublin. He arrived in the capital as a precocious school boy, and left as an experienced orchestra leader and concert soloist. All his basic learning and training was done in Ireland, and the varied knowledge gained in Dublin musical circles stood him well on his travels and later. Like Balfe before him, he had no choice but to move on in order to develop his talents properly. Together with Balfe and that other great musical exile John Field, he made the name of Ireland familiar and popular on the world musical scene. He thus helped to prove that Ireland could produce composers of quality, and home trained at that. Once he left he had little contact with Irish music, though he did arrange and publish selections of Irish tunes such as "An Coilin", the oldest of Irish traditional tunes 'Garryowen' and 'The Harp that Once'. Like the ones arranged by Beethoven and Haydn before him, they were beautifully written, but not at all in character with Irish traditional music form, and so not popular.

Continental Scene

Wallace first toured on the continent in 1844, and returned in 1847 to arrange for a production of MATHILDA OF HUNGARY in Vienna. Since it was based on a Hungarian folk legend, and with a reworked libretto, it was far more successful there, and established Wallace's name. Early in 1848 he returned to produce MARITANA to the plaudits of The Viennese. its string of melodies charmed them, and earned him the title 'King of Melody'. The leading lady of the day, Staudigl played Gitana, which in itself was a compliment to Wallace. No wonder Lortzing and Wagner among others were madly jealous of the intruder. Its Overture was very popular for many years on the continent as a concert piece.

Before the second stage of his operatic career in London Wallace toured widely in Germany and Holland, and it is claimed tht he wrote two operas, GULNARE and OLGA while in Wiesbaden. It is not clear if they ever reached the stage. LURLINE was produced in Germany, but it was naturally overshadowed by Wagner's masterpiece; while in France it was produced as 'La Fille du Rhine'. Wallace's later operas were compared favourably in content and style with those of Auber, then the toast of France. While in Paris during his last illness Wallace's house was a meeting place for no less than Auber, Berlioz and the uncrowned King of the French musical scene, Giocomo Rossini.

World Scene

In some ways Wallace's contribution was greatest one the wider world scene. Certainly it is impossible to name a leading composer or musician who displayed his talents in such diverse, inhospitable and widely spread places. After his Australian and Indian visits he travelled across the immense Pacific Ocean, and gave concerts in many of the capital cities in South and Central America. Even in today's comfortable travelling conditions the amount of ground he covered is enormous; and it should be remembered that in those days there were no railways on that continent, and no roads as we think of them. Yet in spite of his asthma and recurring ophthalmia, Wallace fulfilled his mission of bringing good music well perform to the outskirts of what we call civilization, and for that he was acclaimed and feted all over the world.

It is hardly surprising tht North Americans quickly took to an outgoing character like Wallace; he was tailor-made for their 'gold-fish-bowl' type of living. An extrovert pianist and violinist, a man who composed music that was easy to play and to sing, and who still managed to live life to the full, such a character just had to be lionized by American society. During his first spell there he helped found the New York Philharmonic Symphonic Society and also conducted concerts and opreas in various cities. Next time around he fell in love with a young American based concert pianist; 'married' her although he already had a wife and son he had 'mislaid'; and they toured extensively and successfully as piano-violin duettists.

Although he last set foot in South America in 1849 and departed from North America in 1853, his name and fame lived on. This is shown by the fact that various Wallace operas were later produced in

Cambridge (Mass.), Philadelphia, New Orleans and New York. MARI-TANA even made it to the stage as far away as Cape Town. Certainly his name and fame were familiar to music lovers in all parts of the English speaking world, and his music appreciated.

His place in English Music

While Handel was living in London it was only natural that German opera should hold the stage; and after that period Italian opera dominated. The one English composer to challenge this situation was Thomas Arne whose opera ARTAXERES (1792) was the first local success since the time of Henry Purcell. Arne's opera was composed in the Italian style, and was made up entirely of arias and recitatives. Unfortunately devotees of English opera had to wait forty years for the next success. This was in 1834 when John Barnett's opera THE MOUNTAIN SLYPH was produced.

Dublin born Michael Balfe was the man who lit the fire. He was already an established opera singer of repute, having the previous year sung at la Scala, Milan, with leading soprano Maria Malibran in IL BARBIERRE DE SEVIGLIA, LA CENERENTOLA and OTELLO, three of Rossini's masterpieces. So he arrived in London in 1834 well equipped; a leading singer, a composer, pianist and violinist, with a knowledge of French and Italian. Within a year his name was made when he wrote and sang the leading role, and his wife Lina Roser the female lead, in THE SIEGE OF ROCHELLE at Drury Lane. He wrote nine operas that were staged in London and Paris before his masterpiece THE BOHEMIAN GIRL was written. Balfe composed another twelve operas that were staged in London over the next twenty years, but only THE ROSE OF CASTILLE approached the level of the opera that is forever linked with his name. Strangely, Streatfield in 'The Opera' considers it 'unfortunate for the memory of Balfe that the one opera by which he is remembered, the perennial BOHEMIAN GIRL, is the least meritorious of his many works: it lives solely by reason of the insipid tunefulness of one or two airs'. But he was the saviour of British opera ambitions, and thus a difficult act to follow.

Wallace arrived in London from America in 1844, and the fame and adventures that had stood him so well in the New World made little impression in this cosmopolitan city. As stated the following year in the Illustrated London News: 'Only to concert frequenteres was he at all familiar ... last season when he appeared as a pianist and composer, we were not at all prepossessed in his favour. His playing, compared with the great lion-artists with whom he entered the lists, was anything but electrical. Nor did we trace in any of his compositions, vocal and instrumental, the presence of a master mind'. However in November 1845 the self same critic has a different story to relate after the first production of MARITANA: 'There has been no opera produced for years that has created a greater sensation; the most eminent members of the music profession have attended the performances, and on all hands it is agreed that Wallace is destined to occupy a most prominent position among our native musicians. There are, of course, different opinions as to the extent of his capabilities ..'

Probably to his amazement, Wallace found himself lauded as 'the compeer of Balfe', and possible enjoyed a chuckle or two at his rival's expense. Since leading music critic J.W. Davison offered the opinion in The times:
'Wallace's MARITANA achieved the most complete success ever witnessed within the walls of an English theatre', there can be little doubt of the sensation caused by Wallace. Unfortunately he quickly followed with an opera whose libretto 'is a shining example of the immortal balderdash of the poet Bunn', according to Streatfield, and so missed a golden opportunity of really establishing himself with MATHILDA OF HUNGARY. He compounded his mistake by going to Vienna and spending time there organising performances of these two operas. The Viennese took the Irish rascal to their hearts, and flocked to hear his string of melodies. Even after returning to London Wallace did not get on with his composing career, but took off on another world tour.

Ten years, and many exciting experiences later, Wallace was back in London. Fitzball seized the chance to work with him again, and in February 1860 LURLINE was staged at Covent Garden. According to critic J.W. Klein:
'Unanimously the work was acclaimed as infinitely superior to MARITANA, and it seemed as if English opera might at last be coming into its own ... Unfortunately Wallace had failed to treat his mystical theme with the intense conviction it required, though in any case it was one of the most intractable of subjects'.
Wallace tried in his last three operas to establish an English Opera tradition, but they were more elaborate than the public demanded, and were not successful. Balfe's later opera were similarly criticised, and not sup-

ported either. It seems that both composers had grown musically, but the audiences still demanded ballad operas, or, as it turned out, those of their own home-grown composer, Arthur Sullivan.

Yet, like a ghost form the past, Wallace's operas kept re-appearing on the English stage. During their last three seasons the Pyne Harrison Company staged almost one hundred productions of his operas. In 1873 the Carl Rosa Company began its first season with MARITANA, a significant honour, when you list the choice of English operas available to them. The final season of the Gye era at Covent Garden in 1882 also included MARITANA In 1888 Cornetto de Bassetto (alias G.B. Shaw) wrote a scathing review of a production of LURLINE that he should have known to be unworthy of Wallace's work. At Drury Lane on 1890 the Carl Rosa Company had both MARITANA and LURLINE in the repertory, and at the same theatre in 1892 Augustus Harris also included MARITANA. Even after the turn of the century these two favourites were being produced in provincial theatres. In the early 1890s the derogatory term 'The Irish Ring' was coined to cover the only English operas being regularly produced: Balfe's THE BOHEMIAN GIRL, Wallace's MARITANA, and Benedict's THE LILY OF KILLARNEY. It is ironical that not one of the three composers was born in England, Benedict having been born in Germany.

From the foregoing account, it is clear that Wallace had no inferiority complex as far as English or Irish composers were concerned. He was the recognised compeer of the best in England, and highly thought of in Austria, France and Germany. His skills in melody, harmony inventiveness and orchestration were recognised by one and all.

British Operatic Standards

Professor Dent has referred to this period as:
'The most degrading age through which opera ever passed in England'.
The singer Charles Saintly had described on classical example ' Pare and I were singing a duet when a dog, belonging to the repiteur, trotted onto the stage, and squatted on his haunches in front of me. I was terribly indignant, and tried to drive the beast away with kicks, but he treated me with silent contempt. There he remained until I concluded my cadence, when he rose up, wagged his tail, and walked quietly away'. On another occasion the leading lady, exasperated at the tenor preparing to render a repeat encore, procured a chair from the wings, sat on it

in mid stage, and glared at the singer with unconcealed annoyance. Saintly tells of another interesting scene. 'Honey has a hollow unmusical voice, and knew little about the art of singing, yet he firmly believed that his forte lay in serious song ... he begged me to give him plenty of time to get out a low C in a duet, as it was his great effect; and on a former occasion I had done him out of a round of applause. I promised, but the low C stuck in passage, and would not come out. I walked up and down, waited in exasperation, and when I finally turned around, saw my friend as red as a peony, almost bursting, but not a sound could he produce. The audience took it as a joke, and roared with laughter, to Honey's intense disgust'.

The librettist of LOVE'S TRIUMPH, Planche was insensed enough to publish this letter. ' I cannot pass without a word of reprobation the barbarous treatment to which this opera was subjected, in accordance with common practice in England, but which would not be tolerated elsewhere. Being produced before Christmas, as soon as the holiday arrived it was sacrificed, as too many have been before it, to the pantomime. The length of the dull, monstrous, hybrid spectacle which has superseded the bright, lively and laughable harlequinade of my earlier days, precluded the possibility of giving the opera before it in its integrity. Not only were several airs omitted, but duets and concerted pieces were cruelly hacked and mutilated, without reference to the author or the composer, to the injury of their reputation, and the serious loss to the publishers of the music, who had paid a considerable sum for the copyright'.

The last word can be left with Professor Dent. 'We do wrong at present to apply Grand Opera standards to these romantic operas that were descended from comic operas and not opera seria. The comic element, which comes out very clearly in the spoken dialogue, was the foundation; it is the heroic element which is episodical, for in these operas even heros were allowed to have a sense of humour, at any rate while talking. Their songs seem absurd because the function of music here is to illustrate violent emotion - just the sort of violent emotion which an ordinary Englishman would restrain ... If we find MARITANA and THE BOHEMIAN GIRL laughable on the modern stage, no great harm is done; as a matter of fact an ordinary English audience is always held in tense silence, however old-fashioned the music may be, if the singer has a good voice and sings with conviction. And all tenors sing with conviction, for they are firmly convinced that their own voices are all that matters'.

Financial Constraints

Mere money was of little interest to Wallace, or so it seems. His first business venture in Sydney was gloriously unsuccessful. When he was in America his hard earned wealth was again invested with similar results. After putting much time and effort into rewriting LURLINE he sold the copyright of it for ten shillings, and promptly gave that away. When we read Planche's account of how LOVE'S TRIUMPH was treated by the Pyne-Harrison Company, he must have been financially embarrassed to even think of having another opera, THE DESERT FLOWER, ready for production the next season. And he was working on another one, ESTRELLE, when his health finally gave way in 1864. Confirmation of his poor financial position is given in the 1859 letter to Mrs. Jones. In this he admits owing Nine hundred and seventy six pounds in England and Five Hundred in America; he also claims to have earned less than two hundred pounds in each of the previous five years. While this sounds exaggerated, and probably is, if it is even remotely true, it is a terrible indictment of the slave drivers who were getting rich at his expense.

Satisfying Public Taste

Balfe was the composer who set the standards and established the tastes of the British opera-going public, and during the thirty years from 1835 he wrote over twenty operas that were successful to a greater or lesser degree as time marched on. Wallace also helped carry the flag for British opera, and had six operas produced in the years 1845 - 63. Both composers had travelled extensively on the continent and became influenced by current musical ideas and style. This resulted in their later operas being more stylish and better worked out than their earlier ballad operas, which the two composers had now outgrown. But the paying public would not accept this step up the musical ladder and did not support their efforts. Yet many French operas, on which Balfe and Wallace's later works were modelled, were successfully produced in London at that time. Herold had a number of operas staged, ZAMPA (1831) being the best known. Three at least of Auber's fortysix operas succeeded: MASANIELLO, FRA DIAVOLO, and LE DOMINO NOIR. About twenty of Offenbach's works had successful London productions, among them LE MIRAGE AUX LANTERNES, ORPHEE AUX ENFERS, and MADAME FAVERT, which had over five hundred consecutive performances. French composers of the more elaborate style were also given a good hearing. Halvey's masterpiece LA JUIVE was staged in 1847, and he came to London in 1850 to conduct LA TEMPESTA, based on Shakespeare. The one composer above all that Wallace wished to emulate, Meyerbeer of the spectacular scenes and heroic histrionics, was hugely successful with LES HUGENOTS (1842), LE PROPHETE (1849), DINORAH (1859) and the posthumous opera L'AFRICAINE (1865). Yet when Balfe and Wallace attempted to escape from the straight-jacket of ballad operas with their 'pale simpering maidens, minions, miscreants, traitors and varlets' (Forsyth) the musical public turned their backs on them. Their plight was appreciated and understood by no less than Rossini in Paris, who angrily exclaimed: 'Cochons d'Anglais, Va'; he was outraged by the neglect in their own country of musicians of such great gifts, and realised only too keenly how handicapped an artist can be if he is constantly compelled to go cap-in-hand to impresarios. How lucky were the French and foreign composers to have a sympathetic ear like that of Rossini to fight their cause.

WALLACE - Why no great opera?

After examining all facets of Wallace's life we are left with the key question: 'Why aid Wallace not compose a great opera?. A number of circumstances combined to make it very difficult for him to achieve this ambition.

His Personality and Character:

There are surprisingly few personal details related concerning vincent, and the best account is by his son Willy:
"My father was a wonderful pistol shot, and his nerve and coolness stoood him in very good stead in his many perilous adventures. He was a great horseman, and was very fond of animals, especially dogs, and also fishing, which was his only relaxation in later life. Vincent was about the best tempered and msot amiable man I ever met, and was a tremendous smoker of cigars, a habit he acquired in Havanna and in America. After breakfast he invariably lighted a cigar, and you would hardly see him without one in his mouth till he went to bed. Some friends in Havanna were continually sending him presents of the finest brands, and he did justice to them. He was a particularly temperate man, the only liquor he cared for being good wine."

William Wallace Jnr.

Willy obviously thinks very highly of his father, who seemingly can do no wrong; yet at this time Vincent was living in London with his 'new wife' and sons Clarence and Vincent, having abandoned Willy's mother years previously. Willy appears to have been in closer contact with Vincent than with his mother, and perhaps the reason for this was the precarious state of Alicia's mental health, which was alluded to in Vincent's letter to Anna Kelly.

Vincent believed in living life to the full, and to be a composer beavering away in a lonely garret would be anathema to one of his temperament. Life was for meeting people, seeing places and travelling the world. Like the hero in a Meyerbeer opera, he would have to be in the midst of a mutinous crew or a rebellious tribe of natives. Not satisfied with being London's favourite, he succeeded in making Germany, and above all Austria, applaud him. When he could reel off melodic pieces for the piano, violin or the human voice, why make life any more complicated by striving to compose a masterpiece? At least not yet. Unfortunately the ill-health that had dogged him all his life caught up with him when he turned fifty years of age.

His Education and Training:

Because of family circumstances his personal education was limited, as were his opportunities for musical learning. While he was a young professional musician in Dublin he availed of the best teachers there; but the experience and expertise of these teachers would have fallen patently short of the standard waiting to be absorbed by any would-be-composer on the continent. He probably learned more while leading the Theatre Royal Orchestra, and coping with the tantrums and whims of visiting celebrities. Because of this lack of formal training he never showed the commitment to serious sustained work that was obligatory for him to reach his true potential.

His Librettos and Subjects:

Apart from meeting Fitzball, who had a libretto waiting for the right composer to come along, and Wallace proved to be just that with MARITANA, how much choice had he after that ? The small group of lessees of the opera houses were his only clients; they had to run their productions profitably or go broke (as they did with monotonous regularity); so the kind of opera that would have any chance of being staged would be limited. Balfe had shown the way with THE BOHEMIAN GIRL, a tuneful string of melodies, and he continued in a similar vein for another twenty years. So the path of English opera was set, and it would take a man far more determined than Wallace (a Wagner?) to change its course. Built into the system was the writing of the librettos by the so-called English poets. As critic J.W. Klein wrote: 'The librettos resembled the manufacture of modern television serials, the more involved the story the better ... Their feeble literary efforts were calculated to discourage even the most intrepid pioneer, and they could neither versify competently nor plan a genuinely exciting story.' This view is also expounded by E.J. Dent, who wrote: 'The English operas of this period have become a byword for absurdity, mainly owing to their librettos, especially those written by Bunn and Fitzball. They read as if they were translations, and the reason is that they were imitations of foreign styles ... The English librettists knew exactly what was wanted, but they did not take much trouble about their versification. Probably no one cared in those days if the tunes made nonsense of the words because the poet had carried on the sense from one line to he next without allowing for the inevitable stop at the end of musical phrases'. Another eminent critic, Cecil Forsyth pictures for us a typical stage hero of the time: 'He has a mysterious but admirable way of dealing with the most overwhelming odds; and it must be opined that his own descriptions of these affairs, after the event, are always models of that general circumspection which insists on the recognition of valour without condescending to its petty details. He would describe his prowess to a fragile lady thus:

"But the blade of my sword looked sharp and bright
As I flashed it forth in the dim twilight.
and the miscreants fled with coward wail.
My pretty maiden why turn pale
When we are safe to tell the tale?"

After making his operatic come-back with LURLINE, a dramatic story which brought out the best in Wallace, and earned him favourable comparison with no less than Meyerbeer and Wagner, he picked another dramatic subject in THE AMBER WITCH. He lavished great care on this score, and declared it the best opera he had written. The comparative failure of this opera, after all he had put into it, must have caused Wallace a mental lapse, because it is very difficult to understand how he could have freely chosen such a libretto as THE DESERT FLOWER. Its strange story and improbable characters were unlikely to inspire him to any great heights; perhaps we should charitable assume that he must have been severely constrained financially to have wasted his talents on it.

WALLACE - What is his standing musically ?

When we accept the fact that Wallace never did get to write the great opera he should have composed, we face the difficulty of finding him his rightful place in the hierarchy of music. Since his operatic life was concentrated in London, he should be judged primarily by his influence on the English scene. In his 'Study of English Opera' Cecil Forsyth writes: 'We must judge Wallace's work as we would that of an early

Italian painter, not by the freedom and ease of his successors, but by the stiffness and awkwardness of his predecessors. If we judge Wallace's best work, not by our own standards but by the standards of his English predecessors, we shall be forced to allow it a certain elementary vigour and dramatic spontaneity which were unknown till his day'. Balfe's best loved opera THE BOHEMIAN GIRL appeared in 1843, and Wallace's MARITANA in 1845, and they set the standards of their time. Over the next twenty to thirty years composers such as Verdi and Wagner revolutionised opera composition and production by the detailed care and thoroughness they applied to their scores. Had Balfe and Wallace arrived on the scene twenty years later, their approach would have been less self-indulgent, and they both had the necessary ability and talent to achieve much higher things. Then the great opera could have been written.

Some aspects of Wallace's music influenced even his fellow composers on the continent; after all his operas had been performed in Austria, France and Germany. In Grove VI, Nicholas Temperly wrote: 'The most striking innovation in MARITANA was his use of exotic colouring to illustrate Spanish and Gypsy elements.... These colourings were new, not only in English opera, but in any well known opera; previous operas set in Spanish surroundings, such as LA FAVORITA (1840), DON PASQUALE (1843) and ERNANI (1844) had contained fandangos and boleros, but with orthodox harmonies ... It is hardly fanciful to infer that Wallace absorbed this idiom from the popular music of South America, where he had spent several years; nor is it far fetched to point to a direct influence on Bizet, when one remembers that MARITANA was one of the most successful operas of its generation throughout Europe".

J. W. Klein also notes the CARMEN connection, remarking: 'Then with what an infectious gaiety does a chorus such as "Pretty Gitana" trip along; here Maritana herself comes sparkling to life. In her bewitching "You are to blame" there is a pert charm not altogether unworthy of Bizet himself. For a fleeting instant one is tempted to believe that the composer of CARMEN, and his versatile librettist too, may have cast a cursory glance at this captivating music, and the subsequent "Farewell my gallant Captain". Perhaps these nimble strains haunted Bizet's brain, and conjured up a vision of a subtler, more authentic and far more formidable Gypsy ... It is perhaps difficult to summon up much enthusiasm for the still popular 'Let me like a soldier fall' : but it has certain rumbustious vitality, and may have been partly responsible for the interpolation of Valentine's "Even bravest hearts may swell' into Gounod's FAUST' After all it first appeared, sung by Charles Saintly, when the opera was given in London shortly after its Parisian premiere.

Another situation in MARITANA, the fake execution, was used in a number of later operas. Probably the most dramatic use of the idea was Puccini's in TOSCA when Cavardaossi meets his fate before the incredulous Tosca. Wallace's opera LURLINE ' is based on the lugubrious but immensely popular legend of Lorelei, the romantic mermaid who bewitches her half-demented lovers, but whose lives she is doomed never to share' as Klein explains. The use of this legend, and the placing of one of the scenes in her cave under the Rhine, anticipated Wagner, who later used these ideas to good advantage. All of which shows that Wallace's standing in the European musical scene was considerable indeed during his lifetime.

Wallace in his later years had outgrown the ballad opera frame of mind, and assimilated European ideas on his continental travels. As he explained in a letter to music critic J.W. Davison after his successful visit to Vienna in 1848; 'For my part, I think that music is an art that knows no locality but heaven. Whether one receives its inspirations through an Italian or German medium, I can but think that if the melody is good, the accompaniment correct, and the dramatic sentiment in accordance with the exigencies of the scene, one has attained the end desired, namely to write a good opera'. In his later works the influence of Auber and Mendelssohn can be discerned. But it was the greatest French opera composer of the day, Meyerbeer, that Wallace wished to emulate. A master of the grand heroic spectacular opera, for which Wallace's life story would need no embellishing, Meyerbeer stood supreme in Paris. When Wallace was dying in a castle high in the cloudy Pyrenees, and how appropriate a setting that was after his life of adventure, it was the score of his hero's last opera, L'AFRICAINE (1865), that he was studying. As well as reflecting on the missed musical opportunities of his life, Wallace probably regretted never having has the chance to work with Eugene Scribe, the author of many of Meyerbeer's librettos, who might have inspired him to write the great opera that eluded him. If that had happened, as well as being 'the compeer' of Balfe in England, he would have achieved his life's ambition, to be reckoned the equal of the then King of French opera, Giacomo Meyerbeer.

As Waterford historian Frank Heylin has so aptly expressed it:
'It cannot be said that Wallace's operas were the equal from the musical point of view to those of the Italian masters Rossini, Bellini, Denizetti and Verdi; yet in their own way there was much artistic merit in them, and they were far superior to anything else in these islands of that period. We cannot all rise to the top of the tree, but some of the less high branches are not bad places to be in; and it is no small thing to have composed music that, in its time, went to the heart of thousands of people, and still does. For this reason Wallace is entitled to his place in the Temple of Fame, and in the musical history of Ireland'

On the broader scene, his star no longer shines as brightly as once it did in the constellation of music, as is also true of Michael Balfe and composer-pianist John Field; the three outstanding musicians to be born in nineteenth century Ireland.

William Vincent Wallace was within a grasp of greatness, but failed to take his chance. He will never be ranked among the highest level, the geniuses; neither will he be reckoned among the next echelon, the greats. Wallace's place will be among the next rank, the master craftsmen. It is only by the achievements of these master craftsmen that we realise how wonderful were the greats, and how divinely inspired were the geniuses.

Appendix A

Wallace's Compositions

The notion that Wallace was a lazy idler was inadvertently propagated by his friend the French composer Hector Berlioz. The remark was passed by Berlioz when, referring to the amazing and improbable adventures related by Wallace, he commented: 'Wallace is too lazy to have invented these stories, so they must be true'. In reality Wallace enjoyed creating the impression of being an incorrigible idler, it was part of his mischievous nature. He may not have used all his time wisely, as his detractors naturally do, but he used a great deal of it very well. This is proved by the fact that a list of his works occupies over one hundred pages of the British Music Catalogue in the British Museum.

As listed in Grove VI, the following operas by Wallace were performed:

MARITANA	Drury Lane	1845
MATILDA OF HUNGRY	Drury Lane	1847
LURLINE	Covent Garden	1860
THE AMBER WITCH	His Majesty's	1861
LOVE'S TRIUMPH	Covent Garden	1862
THE DESERT FLOWER	Covent Garden	1863

A number of other operas by Wallace do not appear to have been staged:

THE MAID OF ZURICH	(L. J.E. Carpenter)	1857/8?
THE KING'S PAGE	(L. J.E. Carpenter)	1857/8?
OLGA		1847/8?
GULNARE		1847/8?
ESTRELLE	(L. H.B. Farnie)	1864

THE KING'S PAGE is seldom listed. Given that the librettist and the dates are the same, could it be an alternative name of THE MAID OF ZURICH? Wellington Gurney describes GULNARE and OLGA as 'Italian operas' that were not properly finished, claiming to have heard parts of them in Weisbaden while there with Wallace. Grattan Flood said the composer was in Germany during 1858 and 1859, and is said to have written operas, possibly 'Gulnare' and 'Olga' while in Weisbaden, where they may have been produced. Not all critics agree the 'Estrelle' is the opera Wallace was composing when his health finally failed. Grattan

Flood states that this was the case, and this seems to be confirmed in Grove V which adds: 'the unfinished opera 'Estrelle' was given by Wallace's wife to W.K. Bassard to complete'. Two very interesting questions arise from this: firstly, was the opera ever completed?; secondly, where is it now?

Wallace composed many pieces for his first love, the violin, and performed them very successfully in many parts of the world. Among them were:

Violin Concerto, performed in Dublin 1830
Introduction and Variations: 'La Cracovienne' c.   1835
Grande Valse de Concert
Fantasias and Romances
Arrangements of Irish melodies:
     'The harp that once', 'Fly not yet', etc.   1848
     'An Coolin', 'Garryowen', 'St Patrick's Day'   1859

Wallace was a prolific composer for the piano:

Three Nocturnes
Solos: 'La Gondola', 'La Belle Danceuse'
     'Caprice Heroique', 'Dance Cosaque'
     Grand Fantasia on 'La Cracovienne'
     Little Concert Polka
     Study: 'A Mon Etoile'
     Waltz: 'Sympathy'
Fantasia on   'Lucrezia Bori'   (Donizetti)   1848
     'Rienzi'   (Wagner)   1859
     'Ruin of Athens' (Beethoven)   1860
Transcriptions a la Liszt

There is also a treasure-house of vocal works:

Solemn Mass and Motets written in Thurles in 1830
Grande Missa written and performed in Mexico City 1841
Cantata: 'The Maypole'
Ballads: 'Hope in absence'
     'The Bell Ringer' - favourite of Charles Santley
     'The winds that waft my sighs to thee'
     'The Wood Nymph'
     'The coming if the flowers'
     'Why do I weep for thee' - favourite of Irish soprano
         Catherine Hayes

These are just a selection of the compositions of a concert pianist and violinist who was said to be lazy. When we consider all the concert pieces that he wrote; add to them the ten operas that he composed; allow for his involvement in their production in London and on the Continent; and remember that he was a concert artist and a music teacher, lazy appears to be a slanderous description. In reality it seems far more likely that it was overwork that undermined Wallace's already fragile state of health, his eyesight in particular, and led to his untimely and unfortunate death at the age of fifty three.

Maritana

Text by Edward Fitzball, based on the French play 'Caesar de Bazan' by d'Ennery and Pinel Dumanoir. The words of the songs are by Alfred Bunn. In 3 Acts.

First Production at Drury Lane, London on 15 November 1845
Other productions:

Dublin	1 Jul	1846	Philadelphia	4 May	1848
Edinburgh	15 Dec	1847	New York	6 May	1848
Sydney	19 Apr	1849	New Orleans	Dec	1876
Mexico City		1884	Cape Town		1887

In German (translated by A.J. Becher):

Vienna	8 Jan	1848	Hamburg	16 Feb	1849
Prague		1851			

In Italian (recitatives by Mattei):

Dublin	4 Mar	1877	London	9 Dec	1880
New York	20 Dec	1885			

Revivals:

Brighton	1869;		Carl Rosa, London		1917	
Lyceum	22 May 1925;		Old Vic, 30 Mar 1931			
Waterford		1893,	1912,	1914,	1918,	
		1945,	1973,	1981,	1986.	
Dublin		1943,	1961,	1981,	1986,	1992 C.V.
New York		1948,	1977.			
New York Radio		1945.	Tasmanian Radio		1932.	

Characters:		
	Maritana	Soprano
	Lazarillo	Mezzo-Soprano
	Don Caesar de Bazan	Baritone
	Don Jose de Santarem	Tenor
	King of Spain	Bass

The Stuyvesant Opera Company

presents

MARITANA

an English Operetta
by
William Vincent Wallace

~~Thursday~~, Friday and Saturday Evenings
JUNE ■, 17 and 18, 1977 at 7:30 p.m.
Sunday Afternoon, June 19 at 2:30 p.m.

~~Thursday~~, Friday and Saturday Evenings
JUNE ■, 24 and 25, 1977 at 7:30 p.m.
Sunday Afternoon, June 26 at 2:30 p.m.

presented at

LORETTO THEATRE
20 Bleecker Street (East)
New York, New York
Admission: $3.00

MARITANA in New York

The Times of 15th November, 1845 contains the following notice among the 'Engagements':
"Theatre Royal, Drury Lane
This evening (first time) MARITANA
Charles II, Mr. Borrani: Don Caesar de Bazan,
Mr. W. Harrison: Don Jose de Santarem, Mr. H. Phillips:
Marquis de Montefiori, Mr. H. Horncastle: Marchioness
de Montefiori, Mrs. Selbey: Maritana, Miss Romer.
The etiquette of protocol was evidently more relevant than the importance of the parts. The Marquis and Marchioness, who have very small parts, were deserving of prominence; while no mention was made of the page Lazarillo, not to speak of the composer, librettist, producer or conductor. Wallace himself did in fact conduct the performance."

Review from THE TIMES - Monday 17th November, 1845
        Whoever set the first example in the operatic prelude of introducing melodies that afterwards appear in the opera has created a new species of Overture; a characteristic pot-pourri to prepare the mind of the audience as to what is to follow. Mr. Wallace is one of the modern composers who have perfected this, and his Overture, a brilliant though rambling piece of orchestration, involved some of the most striking of the motifs which he subsequently used.

        "The entry into the introductory chorus 'sing pretty maiden' is a sparkling trifle in the style of Auber. This leads to a charming melody which Miss Romer sang with great taste. Another romance 'Tis the harp in the air' follows and is simple and attractive, and Miss Romer did full justice to this charming morsel. A prayer called 'The Angelus' recalls a similar composition in MAISENELLO by Auber, but cannot compare with it in beauty. A duet 'O fairy wind had I the power' wherein Don Jose artfully encourages Maritana's aspirations, contains some elegant melody and is essentially vocal, a rare merit these days. Don Caesar's solo 'All the world over' shows a wild and reckless character, and Mr. Harrison gave it with all the power and energy needed. The gem of the first act was a chorus interspersed with solos 'Farewell my gallant captain'. The opening is an exquisite pretty melody in the Spanish style, and the flowing melody was deliciously sung by Miss Romer, and the whole was encored with enthusiasm."

        "The second act begins with a ballad for Lazarillo 'Alas those chimes', a sweetly flowing melody supported by an accompaniment of

100

great beauty in which the cello plays a conspicuous part. The character of this song is in perfect feeling with the situation..........and the exquisite singing Miss Poole added to the intrinsic merit of the ballad, and illicited the most spontaneous encore of the evening. A trio 'Turn on old time', which reminds us of DON PASQUALE, involves a lilting melody which at once appeals to the audience. A cavatina by Don Caesar 'Let me like a soldier fall' was vociferated by Mr. Jerez with superabundant energy and the encore was attributed to its sentiments. The ballad 'In happy moments' for Don Jose was inefficiently sung by Mr. Phillips. A pretty chorus 'O what pleasure' and a very unpretending waltz, involving a clever employment of the violins and the cellos, comes next. An aria for the King 'The mariner and his barque' is remarkable for an effective and brilliant obbligato for the violin, played by Mr. Hughes. In the singing of this, Mr. Borrani displays much energy but little finish. In the finale, a charming morceau d'ensemble occurs, remarkable for a very subdued orchestral accompaniment, so infrequent throughout the opera......It must be allowed that there is much gift of writing, great dramatic power and a fund of brilliant orchestration in the finale, far superior to the first act."

"The third act commences with a recitative and aria from Maritana 'Scenes that are brightest' which, replete with melody and sentiment, was sung to perfection by Miss Romer, and encored with zealous unanimity. An aria 'Now my courage', delivered by Mr. Phillips with noisy energy and much ornamentling with gestures, narrowly escaped an encore. A duet for Don Caesar and the King has fine declamatory writing, and evidence of the composer mastering a great quantity of dialogue. A prayer delivered by Maritana and Lazarillo 'Sainted Mother' is characteristic and melodious. Don Caesar's cavatina 'There is flower that bloometh' is a sentimental ballad;...the contest between the "ayes" and the "noes" for an encore was ultimately successful. A troi d'ensemble for the King, Maritana and Don Caesar 'O Maritana' was beautifully harmonised; and the absence of orchestral accompaniment was an agreeable relief. The final cavatina 'With rapture glowing' was vocalised by Miss Romer and offers no available point for criticism. At the fall of the curtain the singers were called for, and subsequently Mr. Wallace, amid long applause."

"We are bound to acknowledge that Mr. Wallace has the disadvantage to wrestle with libretto that would dishearten a composer with less resource and energy....He has courageously striven for the success

101

he has achieved, and is indebted to himself alone. Without being thoroughly original, he possesses an extraordinary flow of ideas which he treats with the knowledge and intelligence of a practised artist. His harmony is bold, varied and musical; in his orchestration he is brilliantly daring, experimental and effective; but occasionally the excessive use of brass instruments smothers the vocal parts. Composers should draw a line more carefully between brilliant orchestration and mere noise. French musicians, with the exception of Auber, continually do this, and produce more noise but infinitely less body and clearness.......We entertain the highest hopes of Mr. Wallace now that he has experience as well as intention at his command. It is a long time since an English opera has been produced, the reception of which was so enthusiastic, and of which so much promise of ultimate eminence was indicated."

It is stated in the Times of 17th November, 1845:

'The immense success of Wallace's opera, which was received on Saturday with perfect enthusiasm by a house literally crammed to the ceiling, ensures that it will be repeated every evening'. So popular was MARITANA that is quickly achieved its fiftieth performance on 5th February, 1846, an event celebrated with a benefit for Wallace with a concert at Covent Garden. Within a week he was in Dublin for a concert version at the Rotunda Concert Hall attended by everyone from Lord Lieutenant downwards. It was almost five months before the full Drury Lane Company arrived.

Review in 'The Freeman's Journal' of 2nd July, 1846:
"Wallace's very successful opera MARITANA was produced last evening for the first time in Dublin. He is a composer of very decided merit and it makes us not a little proud to have the author as a countryman. It has been very well put upon the stage in our Theatre Royal, and the musical arrangements are very creditable to Mr. Levey."

"The Overture contains some pleasant passages with harp accompaniment at the commencement. There are also several themes for the violin. It will be remarked that it contains most of the themes we later hear in the opera."

"Were we to offer an opinion as to the most attractive morceaux, we should name: 'Tis the harp' with its delicious arpeggios; the fine cavatina 'Let me like a soldier fall'; and the hymn 'Sainted Mother'. Nor could we forget the trio 'Turn on old time', in which the concept is at once dramatic and original; Don Caesar chiding the slowness of the time which has to elapse before his execution; the page, Lazarillo responds with wishes that time's progress could be retarded; and Don Jose interrupts at the close of their verses with an offer of safety on certain conditions. We do not think it necessary to give a full stretch of the plot, especially as we have said in our last notice that it is almost identical with the play Don Caesar de Bazan."

"We have in the opera, as in the drama, a hero condemned to die for fighting a duel during Holy Week; he is saved in the same manner by the page. The same cross-purpose of court intrigue to favour the designs of Don Jose upon the Queen, and of the King on Maritana, are introduced and bring the plot to the same denouement."

"We are very happy to report the Miss Romer has completely shaken off the cold under which she appeared to labour on her first appearance, and that her voice was in the usual excellent order. There is a delicious thrill pervading her intonation in loud passages which reminds me of the words of the poet "clear as a trumpet, but with silver sound". Mr. Harrison was in excellent voice, and gave his songs with great effect. We were particularly pleased with the simple sweetness of his singing during 'There is a flower' and in 'Turn an old time'. We must not omit to speak of Miss Holmes who sang her part in this charming trio with judgement and sweetness. Mr. Borrani was as usual most effective; he was encored for 'In happy moments', a song, the words of which (by Alfred Bunn), have been most humorously criticised by Punch magazine."

"The opera was announced for repetition every evening this week. The house was full and fashionably attended every night since the opera opened."

Report from 'The Freeman's Journal' - 6th July, 1846:
'Last night we witnessed another performance of MARITANA with increased pleasure. The performance has improved with repetition. The trio 'Turn on old time' is a delicious morceaux. We omitted from our last notice to mention the careful and correct performance of Mr. Corri; it was a very useful and painstaking effort'.

Report from 'Saunder's Newsletter':
'A most favourable estimate must be formed of the genius of the

composer, our gifted countryman.....Mr. Wallace has done much indeed for his reputation, and we look with anxiety to his future productions'.

It is worth noting that during the visit to Dublin of the Drury Lane Company, five performances of MARITANA were given, one of BOHEMIAN GIRL, one of LA SONNAMBULA, and one comprising THE ENCHANTRESS followed by the first act of LA SONNAMBULA. So this was no make-shift outfit, but an experienced opera ensemble. On each occasion the operatic programme was followed by a face with such interesting titles as 'The Spectre Bridegroom' and 'Did you ever send your wife to Kingstown'. After 9.30 p.m. there was a second admission price to some parts of the house. A visit to the Theatre really was a night out in those days.

William Vincent Wallace Centenary 1912

Reports in 'Waterford News' - November 1912:

"On Thursday 14th November, 1912 at the Large Room, City Hall, Dr. Grattan Flood, Mus. Doc. N.U.I., gave a lecture entitled 'A Centenary Celebration'. Dr. Flood illustrated the lecture by playing some of Wallace's beautiful but lesser known works, such as THE AMBER WITCH and LURLINE. From the latter opera Irish soprano Miss Agnes Treacy sang 'Sweet spirit hear my prayer' and Mr. Tom Reddy 'A Father's love'. Mr. Reddy also rendered the stirring ballad 'The Bell Ringer' to an appreciative audience.

"Another highlight of the Centenary Celebrations was a 'Maritana Ball' in City Hall. For this Mr. Harris Rosenburg and his Band were specially engaged. Members of the Maritana Company attended in their costumes. Not to be outshone, members of the public could hire spare costumes, supplied my Messers Burkenshaw of Liverpool, at 5s. each. Admission cost 5s 6p for a Gent and 3s 6p for a Lady.

Centenary Performance of MARITANA:

"The company of Waterford amateurs which Dr. Storer led through MARITANA astonished the eminent tenor Mr. Harry Beaumont at the dress rehearsal, and certainly more than astonished the vast audience assembled last night. From the first chorus all were rendered with precision, expression and firmness of attack, and the admirable manner in which all members of the Chorus went through their moves on stage reflects the highest credit on Mr. Goggin, the stage manager.

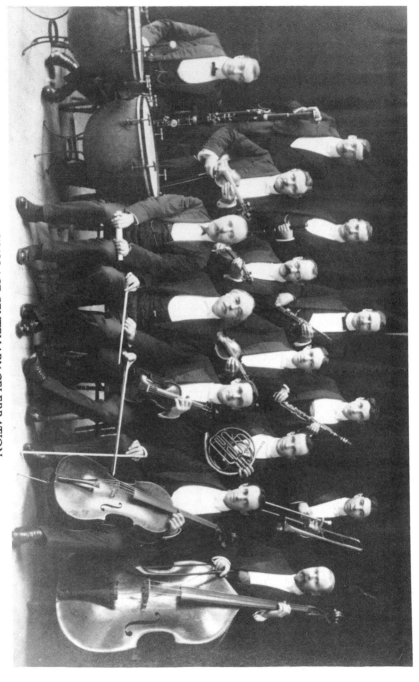

WALLACE CENTENARY CELEBRATION
Performance of Maritana at Waterford November 20th-22nd 1912 Orchestra

"Little need be said of the Don Caesar of Mr. Harry Beaumot; from such an experienced artist it is only necessary to say that it was admirable. Mrs. Smullen made a most spirited and bright Maritana, expressing the music of this trying part exceedingly well. Of Miss Cullen as Lazarillo, we can only say that a more perfect Lazarillo would be difficult to imagine, and her beautiful voice was best heard in 'Alas those chimes'; while her duet with Mrs. Smullen, 'O Sainted Mother' was exquisite. Mr. Tom Manahan as Don Jose gave a worthy performance both from the acting and the singing point of view. The part of the King of Spain was regally played by Dr. Hogan, who made not only a most gracious and polished monarch, but also sang the music with great finish.

"Right through, the singing of the chorus was first rate. 'The Angel's Chorus' and the finale to Act 1 and Act 2 were magnificently sung. As for the orchestra, certainly an opera has not been heard in Waterford accompanied as MARITANA has been. Wallace's delicate orchestration was brought out in every detail under the leadership of Mr. Harry McCarthy; the whole being under Dr. Storer's experienced baton, and was rendered in a manner that in itself was worth going to the theatre to hear.

CAST:		
	Maritana	Mrs. B. Smullen
	Lazarillo	Miss M. Cullen
	Don Caesar de Bazan	Mr H. Beaumont
	Don Jose de Santarem	Mr T. Manahan
	King of Spain	Dr. Hogan
	Marchioness de Montefiori	Mrs. Larkin
	Marquis de Montefiori	Mr. J. Manahan
	Captain of the Guard	Mr. W.J. Browne
	Alcade	Mr. J.B. Downes
	Boatman	Mr. W.J. Long
	Nobleman	Mr M. Murray
	Premiere Danceues	Miss Ashworth
	Musical Director	Dr. John Storer Mus. Bac.

ORCHESTRA:
1st Violins	H. McCarthy	W.E. Meredith
2nd Violins	J.J. Pierce	T. Brabazon
Violas	G.D. Croker	J.A. McCoy

Cello	C.B. Meredith	Double Bass	E.G. Batts
Oboe	T.A. Longmire	Flute	H.J. Hunt
Clarinet	T. Jones	Bassoon	J. Walsh
Horn	J. Doyle	Trombone	T. Gordon
Tympani	W.C. Mercer	Piano	R. Ashworth

Matilda Of Hungary

Text by Alfred Bunn, based on European folk legend. First performance on 22nd February, 1847 at Drury Lane.

Characters:		
	Queen Matilda	Soprano
	Lilla	Contralto
	Attendant to Queen	Soprano
	King Ladislav)	
	Paribrad)	Baritone
	Count Magnus	Tenor
	Innkeeper	Bass

Review in 'THE TIMES' - 23rd February, 1847:

"Mr. Wallace's first opera MARITANA gained a forbearing for its composer that is not to be maintained by second effort of inferior merit......It is pleasant for us to record the success of MATILDA OF HUNGARY, success not only uncontested, but based upon more solid grounds than that of MARITANA, and with an equal profusion on the evidence reflected in the score of his second opera, leading to a much higher school of writing than that of his first score."

"The story of MATILDA OF HUNGARY is founded upon an incident in Bohemian history which itself bears the strongest marks of improbability, and has been so clouded in romance that it is not easy to arrive at the real truth. King Ladislav has perished in battle against the Turks, but the populace are not convinced of his death. The Chief Minister, Count Magnus, has designs on the hand of the Queen to establish his position, but is rejected by her. Magnus finds a young man Paribrad who is the image of the late King, and tries to put the young man in Ladislav's place, and to thus control the throne. Paribrad confesses his imposition to the Queen, and Magnus is foiled."

"Improbable as are the incidents of this story, Mr. Wallace manages to turn it to good account; the incongruities of the plot are forgotten in the splendid scenic allusions with the addition of agreeable melodies and brilliant orchestral devices. The Overture, without aiming at profundity, interests by the appearance of its form and the effectiveness of his instrumentation. Some of the most attractive melodies in the opera are used for subjects, and the variety given them by the orchestral colouring adds to their intrinsic beauty. The fragmentary character of many modern Overtures, of which Mr. Wallace gave a good example in MARITANA, are here used to advantage."

"The first Act contains several pieces worthy of special notice. A song by Mathias, the Innkeeper 'His standard was raised', sung by Mr. Boyce with great spirit, was encored. The violins added character suitable to the legend, and the cellos, which varied the instrumentation of the second couplet, are worthy of note; and the responsive chorus in the major key serves as a good contrast. A ballad for Paribrad, excellently sung by Mr. Harrison, is a melody at once agreeable and original, set off by a pleasing accompaniment a la bolero, in which the flutes and clarinets are effectively employed......An air for Count Magnus 'She comes in all her loveliness' commences with a pretty clarinet solo, but hardly carries out the promise it affords; and Mr. Borrani's heavy style of singing did not improve things. A duet for the Queen and Count Magnus is remarkable for its lovely melodic cantabile phrase a la Spohr, which occurs in the first part, and a cabaletta which has all the spriteliness of the Italian school. A duet for Paribrad and Magnus 'Before the Queen we kneel' has some charming points of orchestration; and a ballad for Paribrad 'Adieu fair land' is a simple melody with harp accompaniment of appropriate unpretentiousness, for which Mr. Harrison receives another encore. The finale to the first act is a picturesque and dramatic illustration of the immediate points of action in the story. A similar situation might have suggested to Mr. Wallace the magnificent finale of the second act of Rossini's WILLIAM TELL as a model, but it is only just to say that he disregarded this, and relied solely on his own resources, which make his success all the more honourable."

"The second act is heralded by a clever instrumental movement in which the violin has a brilliant obbligato, while the clarinet executed a quaint and abley sustained figure. The air for the Queen contains an andante and a striking florid rondo, which was well sung by Miss Romer, and encored. The dance and chorus 'This happy day we celebrate' has an air of nationality about it that is in character with the plot. The march which accompanies the splendid procession in honour of the returned King is very characteristic, but suffers from a wanton variety of instrumentation. An exceedingly pretty barcarolle for Mr. Harrison 'Like waves which o'er' the ocean' suffered materially from poor accompaniment. The next ballad for Magnus 'Gone by that crime' is one of the melodic tunes of the opera; its unobtrusive beauty, and the natural and unaffected manner in which it was rendered by Mr. Harrison, won a deserved encore. A pleasing chorus for female voices 'Thy fondest wishes' is followed by a gloomy air for the Queen 'They who would still be happy'. A duet for the Queen and Paribrad 'This deep affront' is written in the modern Italian style, but has little to recommend it. The finale contains a morceau d'ensemble for the five principal characters which is well written and effective. The accompaniment, being confined to a single flute and the bass in pizzicato, contrasts agreeably with the incessant use of the full orchestra up to that point."

"The third act opens with an accompaniment recitative for Lilla, sung by Miss Litraco, which is plaintive and beautiful; the winning notes of the violin giving happy expression to the sentiments of the melody. This leads to a pretty ballad in the Swiss style 'A lovely youth, a mountain child' which Miss Isaacs, with her fresh voice and unassuming manner, sing so pleasingly as to win an encore. A similar compliment was paid to Miss Romer in the very elegant and expressive romanza 'That devotion in which we breathe' which the fair singer interpreted with utmost feeling. The trio for Magnus, Paribrad and Mattias was one of the most ably written pieces in the opera. It reminds us of Spohr, but the subject and its general development are entirely original."

"The opera has been produced with evident care, and the scenery and appointments are of a gorgeous character that recalls the days of GUSTAVUS III and other opera spectacles famous in the annals of Drury Lane. "The Valley of Thabor" is a picturesque mountain scene in Mr. Grieve's best style, and was acknowledged by a large burst of applause; similar compliments were accorded to, and equally deserved by "The Bridge and Palace of Prague" and "The Grand Hall of the State of Bohemia". At the fall of the curtain the principal singers, then Mr. Wallace who had presided in the orchestra, and Mr. Bunn himself, were called on stage for a wonderful reception. With a few curtailments, not of music but of detail, the opera will go all the better. There can be little doubt of its benefiting the establishment, and of it acquiring popularity with the public."

Review in 'The Illustrated London News':

"The second opera by the composer of MARITANA was produced on Monday night with decided success.....The first question that suggests itself is whether the new production is the equal of MARITANA. It is scarcely fair to institute this comparison, for Wallace's first opera was a comic or buffo opera, and his present work is an opera seria.....As a musician his fame must be increased by MATILDA OF HUNGARY, the third Act of which is as fine as anything can be in the way of fertile imagination and elaborate treatment; still on the whole, there is greater charm and more completeness about MARITANA. But we must take into account that MARITANA was infinitely better acted than MATILDA. Miss Romer excepted, nothing could be worse played than the parts of Borrani, Harrison and Weiss; their characters, in the hands of skilful actors, would have told immensely. "

Lurline

Libretto by Edward Fitzball. In 3 Acts.

First Performed: 23rd February, 1860 at Covent Garden

	Dublin	30 Apr 1861	Sydney	Sep 1862
Also:	Cambridge Mass. USA (Concert Ver.)	1 Jan 1863	New York	13 May 1869 in English 14 May 1863 in Italian (tr. G. Vacotti)

In German: Konigsberg Feb 1863

French Edition pub. as LORELI ou LA FILLE DU RHONE

Revived:	Liverpool	22 Jan 1890
	Drury Lane	12 Apr 1890
	And in the provinces as late as 1927	
	Dublin	1937

Characters:	Lurline Nymph of the Rhine		Soprano
	Liba	Her attendant	Contralto
	Ghiva	Baron's Daughter	Mezzo-soprano
	Count Rudolph		Tenor
	Rhineberg	King of Rhine	Baritone
	Baron		Bass
	The Gnome		Bass

Covent Garden Archives - 24th February, 1860:

"At the Royal English Opera the success of Wallace's new opera LURLINE, produced in the complete and effective manner which has honourably distinguished every public effort of the Pyne Harrison management, exceeded even the most sanguine expectations. At the first representation of this important and complicated work, in which band, chorus and principal singers are allotted tasks of equal responsibility, the performance last night may stand comparison with any on record."

"No less than seven pieces were redemanded and repeated; many of the encores being so genuine and spontaneous that even though they inconveniently protracted the duration of the performance, they could not in courtesy have been declined. Numbers thus marked out for distinction were: the Overture; the bacchanalian chorus for men 'Drain the cup of pleasure'; the song by Miss Pilling 'Troubador Enchanting'; the ballad for Santley 'The nectar cup may yield delight'; the ballad for Harrison 'My home, my heart's first home'; and the unaccompanied four-part song for Pyne, Cruise, Santley and Corri. Other pieces, too many to repeat here, were received with an extraordinary degree of favour at the end of each set. After the customary compliments had been paid to the chief performers, Wallace was summoned with acclaim to the footlights, and crossed the stage amid plaudits that it seemed would never cease."

THE TIMES - 3 March 1860
"We have mentioned previously that Wallace's new opera LURLINE had been produced at Covent Garden with complete success, a success no greater than it deserved. For the composer has mounted a challenge which compares favourably with the best German, French or Italian dramatic musicals of the present day. The music, however excellent as it is, suffers from a libretto which has all the faults of the productions of English playwrights."

"It is one of the fine old legends of the Rhine ... Lurline is a water-nymph, possessed of power and irresistible fascination, which implies the destruction of men, leading them to their fate with spells and incantations. She is a woman, nevertheless, though a sort of fiend, and loves a mortal with a woman's love. She lures him into the Rhine, but instead of letting him perish beneath the waves she conveys him to her cave of coral beneath the waters. After a time she allows him to revisit

111

his home, accepting his pledge to return. But he forgets his water-nymph, and is about to be married, when Lurline's magic makes the river rise and sweep away her faithless lover, his castle and all that belongs to him."

"But this terrible catastrophe, though the essence of the tale, is avoided by the playwright. It turns the demon of the Rhine into a romantic young lady, and the unfaithful Baron into a compliant lover, and makes them happy at last in the bonds of matrimony. Add to this the usual garnish of stupid comic characters, and you have a melodramatic dish cooked in the approved style of our cockney cuisine. We are sorry for this, for the subject, in its own simplicity, is eminently capable of inspiring the genius of a musician like Wallace. Under the disadvantage of having to deal with a quantity of thrash, he has used everything good left in the subject to the most admirable account, and has produced music beautiful, impressive and picturesque such as might have been written by Wagner or Mendelssohn. Such music cannot be described to be appreciated, it must be heard; and readers within reach of Covent Garden have the means of hearing it to perfection."

"We have seldom seen an opera more splendidly got up or more admirable performed. There is no room or fine acting, the characters being reduced to the merest commonplace. The terrible nymph of the Rhine turns out to be an agreeable and interesting young lady, and is made such by Miss Louise Pyne, who is raised above the level of ordinary mortals by the beauty of the strains which she sings. The hero is a walking gentleman, and Mr. Harrison walks well and sings superbly. Mr. Santley acts the part of the Rhine King a character which affords no room for dramatic talent, but there is some fine music in the part which, we need scarcely add, he sings beautifully. There are two stupid characters, meant to be comic, which are played by Mr. Whitty and Miss Pilling. This clever young lady sings a pretty ballad with such harmony that it is encored. The orchestra and chorus do everything that could be desired, and the scenery and decorations are rich and beautiful."

LONDON MUSIC IN 1888-89 by Cornetto de Bassetto:

"I heard LURLINE for the first time. Evidently indeed for the first time; since if I pretended that, having before heard Wallace's masterpiece, anything short of being in love with one of the performers could have induced me to go again, I should not be believed by any expert. No, once is enough, if not too much."

"And yet there are several moments in the opera in which the string of hackneyed and trivial shop ballad stuff rises into melody that surges with genuine emotion. During the first half of the Overture you say to yourself "Now, if he can only keep this up, LURLINE will come out at the head of modern English operas". But he does not keep it up; and presently you are wallowing in banalities that are fully worthy of the desperate thrash, the naked and unashamed nonsense, of Fitzball's libretto. If Wallace had taken his art seriously, he would no more, in his mature age, have set a line of such fustian to music, than Wagner would have turned aside from the score of PARCIFAL to set Scribe's ROBERT LE DIABLE. And the poor silly public forgave Wallace for the sake of "Sweet spirit, hear my prayer", just as they would make much of that other absurdity THE BOHEMIAN GIRL for the sake of "When other lips" and "I dreamt that I dwelt in marble halls".

"I cannot say that the performance was much less ridiculous than the piece itself. Obviously a good deal might be done with the Rhine scenery, and the changes from the depths of the river to its surface. The problem of making Lurline look like a water sprite without exposing her to an undue risk of catching cold is also one for a costumier of genius."

"Madame Burns secured a great success as Lurline. In the concerted piece in the last scene of Act 2 she had much to contend against. The brass blared; Mr. Lely roared; Mr. Crotty shouted; Mr. Eugene bellowed; the chorus also lent a willing hand; but Madame Burns was able for them all. She sent her voice ripping, tearing, piercing through the hurly-burly until the gallery, astounded, and almost hysterical, madly demanded a repetition of the unparalleled sensation. It was magnificent, but it was not singing. However, it brought down the house; if that is all Madame Burns cares for, I have only to congratulate her on her entire success. her other efforts were comparatively lustreless. The first lines of "Sweet spirit, hear my prayer" were not ill sung; but "Take this cup of sparkling wine" was given in a fashion which in London is generally confined to the music hall; and the shakes (trills) which she introduced were made up of wrong notes - not even the right notes sung flat - but actually of notes far removed from those which she intended to sing."

"Mr. Crotty sang his ballad in Act 2 very well, and the hearty encore he got was the heartiest of the evening. Mr. Lely got on fairly as

Rudolph the ridiculous; but Mr. Eugene, whether his cramped posture disabled him, or whether his Neptune-like beard got into his mouth, could do nothing with the florid passages in the drinking song. Not that it mattered; the song is not worth singing well, because it is not worth singing at all."

"The work will be repeated on Tuesday, on which occasion I shall make a point of being elsewhere."

It is interesting that in his critical biography published shortly after Wallace's death, French music critic Arthur Pougin only analyses one opera in detail, LURLINE. After suggesting that the subject is banal and trite, he remarks that 'the work is lacking neither in grandeur nor grace, neither charm nor poetry, and lends itself to a musical setting'. He sees influences of Weber's OBERON in the Overture; 'it is modulated with uncommon cleverness, orchestrated with pomp, and splendidly constructed'. But there is a lack of unity in the score. 'In this respect this adorable work offends. it lacks a "sui generis", a personal style: so exact at depicting the sentiments which it expresses so happily ... LURLINE is an extremely remarkable, if incomplete work; elegant to a supreme degree, quite appropriate to the exigencies of the scene. But the style is composite'. There appears to be so much that is good in the opera, yet all these faults are paraded out.

In his appraisal of Wallace, Pougin maintained that he was always learning from his contemporaries no less than from his predecessors. It was his respect for their talents that made him inclined to be over-derivative. His well attested modesty was also a contributory factor.

THE AMBER WITCH

Text by H.F. Chorley, founded on the novel 'Die Bernsteinexe' by W. Mienhold. In 4 Acts.

First Produced on 28th February 1861 at His Majesty's Theatre but transferred shortly afterwards to Drury Lane.

Revived at Southport 12th January 1899, Clapham, London 22nd March 1899.

CHARACTERS:

Elsie, Servant to Commandant	Soprano
Rudiger, Lord of Ravenstein	Tenor
The Commandant	Baritone
The Pastor of Cosrow	Bass
Klaus, a half-witted Postman	Tenor
The King	Bass

Review in THE TIMES - 1 March 1861

At His Majesty's Theatre Wallace's new opera in 4 Acts, entitled THE AMBER WITCH, to a libretto by Chorley, was produced last night in the presence of a densely crowded house, and was a complete success. The principal singers, Mdm. Lommens-Sherrington, Miss Huddart, Messers Patey, Santley and Simms Reeves were recalled after every act. At the conclusion of the opera similar compliments were paid to Mr. Charles Halle, the conductor, who had thoroughly earned it; for a more efficient first performance of a new and difficult work has rarely been heard.

The music is almost as complicated as it is beautiful, and too much praise can hardly be accorded to the orchestra and the chorus under Mr. Halle's control, both having been materially reinforced for the occasion. The house was enthusiastic in demonstrations of approval, the applause was incessant, and many pieces were redemanded. The singers, in emulation of the example recently set by Simms Reeves, invariable and respectfully declined the honour.

Review in THE ATHENAEUM:

Since he had written the libretto, H.F. Chorley could hardly be too critical, and so commented:
"Some attempt has been made to follow Dr. Meinhold's novel, and the incidents are similar to but more intense than those of Rossini's LA GAZZA LADRA. It is a pity that the composer disregarded the librettist's protests and introduced a sprightly rondo after a peculiarly tense situation. The music is the most elaborate English serious opera which has yet been produced, Wallace having bent himself to try conclusions with writers as able and intricate in their stage-effects as Halevy, Meyerbeer and others at the Grand Opera of Paris. All concerned are to be complimented for the evenness and excellence of the performance,

though the smallness of the stage handicapped them."

The bitterness of Chorley's feeling over Wallace changing the libretto is underlined by the appearance of a report in 'The Athenaeum' within a month of the composer's death in 1865:

"We are instructed that THE AMBER WITCH, arranged as an opera by H.F. Chorley, will be re-set for Continental performance, and that the book will be restored to its original form. Certain interpolations introduced by Wallace, in defiance of the author's protests, and accepted only from deference to the publishers, will be removed. As the opera now stands, the heroine is in every one of her great situations, smothered by being thrown into concerted music, her part being thereby blurred and rendered inneffective. It was Wallace's peculiarity to occupy himself with details rather than the outline of a story or character, and yet to indulge himself in any concession to the folly of his artists. Thus there is no end of contradictions to sense and probability in both book and music".

It would be interesting to speculate on whether the libretto of THE AMBER WITCH was re-written, if the new version ever reached the stage, and whether or not it was more successful than Wallace's. Sadly we don't know.

THE MAPLESON MEMOIRS 1888

"During 1860 negotiations were entered into with Macfarren for the production of a new English work entitled ROBIN HOOD, to a libretto by Oxenford. This opera met with very great success, and the attention of the public was directed towards it even when other works were performed."

"I also opened negotiations with Vincent Wallace to prepare a new opera to follow. It was entitled THE AMBER WITCH, with a libretto by Chorley. In it were Simms Reeves, Mdm. Lommens-Sherrington, Santley, Patey and others ... It was thought advisable to transfer THE AMBER WITCH from His Majesty's Theatre to Covent Garden. (Because of another of the perennial financial crises in opera circles). The wardrobe belonging to the opera, which had somehow fallen off the portico of His Majesty's Theatre on a Sunday morning, found its way to Drury Lane Theatre. Here the part of the Amber Witch was again undertaken by Madame Lommens-Sherrington."

STUDENT AND SINGER by Charles Santley.

For the 1860-61 season at His Majesty's Theatre there was a production of Macfarren's ROBIN HOOD to open the season, and Wallace's THE AMBER WITCH to close it. ROBIN HOOD, in which Simms Reeves returned to the stage after some years absence, was a success. THE AMBER WITCH, though it contained some fine music, was not. I sang it at Drury Lane for some two or three weeks after its production at His Majesty's had closed, to almost empty benches.

At one rehearsal of THE AMBER WITCH the Stage Manager showed off to peculiar advantage. In the last act, the so-called witch, finding herself menaced by a number of peasants who believe her to be a sorceress, conceives the idea of acting on their superstitions, and she sings or recites Latin prayers. This the peasants take for a spell, and hurry away, leaving her in peace. On hearing the prayers, the Stage Manager called out: "Don't you hear she is praying, get down on your knees". I happened to know the situation from reading Chorley's libretto, and took it upon myself to point out the mistake. The Stage Manager merely remarked: "How the devil should I know anything about it, I never read the book". He continued "Hear you chorus: its a spell to frighten you; so as soon as you hear the first words, clear off the stage as fast as you can".

LOVE'S TRIUMPH

Libretto by J.R. Planche (James Robinson) In 3 Acts.
First Produced: 3rd November 1862 at Covent Garden.
CHARACTERS:

Princess de Valois)	Soprano
Therese)	
Attendant to Princess	Mezzo-Soprano
Adolphe	Tenor
Marquis de Pons	Baritone
Count de Canilac	Bass

(Review from the Illustrated London News)

In this work Wallace has the co-operation of the distinguished veteran J.R. Planche, whose libretto is worth in every way of its accomplished author. The subject is gay and comic; the dialogue elegant and lively; and in the lyrical portions adorned with the graces of poetry. Mr. Planche states that the idea of the opera was suggested by a comedy "La Portrait vivant", produced at the Theatre Francaise some twenty years ago. But this obligation amounts to nothing more than confusion of identity, caused by the personal resemblance of two female characters, strangers to each other in all other respects. But even this point is differently treated in the two pieces, and the drama in all essential parts is Planche's own.

"A young provincial nobleman, Adolphe by name, comes to Paris to obtain employment at the Court of the Regent, the Duke of Orleans. He has been recommended by the Duke of Pons, a nobleman, by whom he is presented to Princess de Valois, the Regent's daughter. Adolphe is a disconsolate lover, and seeing in the Princess the living likeness of his distant love, he commits extravagances of behaviour which do him no harm in the Princesses's eyes. While he is growing in the Court's favour, his beloved Therese is brought to Paris by her father, by whom she has been betrothed to a spendthrift nobleman, who wishes to retrieve his ruined fortune by a wealthy marriage. Thus the presence of the two ladies, so much alike that nobody can distinguish between them, produces the series of mistakes, perplexities and cross-purposes which form the plot of the piece."

"Miss Louise Pyne personates both ladies; a quaint and amusing effect is produced by the cleverness with which she passes from one character to the other; appearing one moment as Therese, ad the next as the Princess; the same person but different in dress, deportment and manner. Adolphe is an ordinary stage lover, sighing like a furnace, and singing pretty ballads. The Marquis is an intriguing courtier, who is jealous of Adolphe's advancement. This character is admirable drawn and acted by Mr. Harrison, whose lively picture of a noble roue of the most professional Court in Europe, heartless and unprincipled but polished and elegant, is wittily played. There is a pleasant sketch of a saucy Court page, embodied with much archness and vivacity by Madame Laura Baxter. Count de Canilac is a very insipid personage, on whom Mr. Weiss's talents, both as an actor and a singer, are thrown away."

"As a musical work this is at last the equal, perhaps in some respects superior,to any of Wallace's previous operas; though we doubt if he has ever excelled his first essay MARITANA . In LOVE'S TRIUMPH there is a great deal of the French style: in writing it he has visions of the Opera Comique. It is light, gay and sparkling, and strongly reminds us of Auber, though we cannot charge Wallace with any studied intonation of that, in many respects, inimitable composer. The concerted pieces are particularly excellent; they are constructed with masterly clearness, and carry the action of the scene with unflagging animation and spirit. Among the airs and ballads are some evidently intended (according to the European fashion of opera writing: chiefly for the music ships; but there are others which are as appropriate as they are beautiful."

"Among those which made the greatest impression were: the Overture, a most brilliant and dramatic prelude which was loudly encored; the air "Though all the poor", excellently sung by Mr. Perren as Adolphe; the music of the festive dance in Act 1, singular, graceful and beautiful; the little air 'I'm a model page' sung by Madame Baxter with great vivacity and archness; a grande scena sung by Miss Pyne in Act 11, 'O rank thou hast thy shackles', a magnificent composition which displayed all her powers of voice, execution and impassioned expression; a charming unaccompanied part-song 'Concern for Cleora dying' which cannot fail to gain unbounded popularity; and Miss Pyne's bravura passage in the finale, which brought down the house."

"We need scarcely add that the opera was got up with all the care, completeness and splendour which characterises the management of the Pyne-Harrison Company; and that the performance was received with enthusiastic applause, with repeated calls for the composer and the principals. All the indications are for a brilliant success."

Review from the DAILY TELEGRAPH:
"To the question of what genre does this work belong; it is emphatically a comic opera, with a sufficient tinge of romance to give it a deeper interest. Though the music is light, sparkling and brilliant throughout, the work would be improved by the excision of every solo not needed to carry on the action. Although he modified the denouement of the story, Planche's dialogue is smart and brilliant, and his verse more polished and elegant than most words written for operas".

119

RECOLLECTIONS AND REFLECTIONS by Planche.

"In November 1863 my opera of LOVE'S TRIUMPH, the music by Vincent Wallace, was produced at covent Garden. I cannot pass without a word of reprobation the barbarous treatment to which this opera was subjected, in accordance with common practice in England, but which would not be tolerated elsewhere. Being produced before Christmas, as soon as the holiday arrived it was sacrificed, as too many have been before it, to the pantomime."

"The length of the dull, monstrous, hybrid spectacle which superseded the bright, lively and laughable harlequinade, precluded the possibility of giving the opera before it in its integrity. Not only were several airs omitted, but duets and concerted pieces were cruelly hacked and mutilated, without reference to the author or the composer, to the injury of their reputation. And serious loss to the publishers of the music, who had paid a considerable sum for the copyright, and were thus deprived of the advantage they had counted upon from the nightly singing of these airs, which were omitted, not for want of merit, but for lack of time. And this remember, by a management which solicited the support of the public for a National Opera. "

STUDENT AND SINGER by Charles Santley

"Until the production of Wallace's opera LOVE'S TRIUMPH in November 1863, the operas of the repertoire were successfully played. The new opera was not a success; the music and the libretto were both charming; but the stage of Covent Garden was too large a frame for the picture, and there was a lack of elegance about the whole mise-en-scene which destroyed the brilliance of the work. I believe it would have been a great success if it had been played with spirit in a theatre such as the Prince's, where the dialogue could have been spoken more rapidly than in a large theatre."

"I had declined to sing the baritone part; it was of no importance dramatically or musically, the only number being a ballad introduced to make weight, appros of nothing in particular. When the opera was not a success I was sorry I had refused the part, as Wallace was a good friend of mine; although I could not have done anything with such a part to render him any service ... The only part that I refused was in LOVE'S TRIUMPH, and had it not been that I was much in need of a rest I do not think I would have refused it. The average season was of five months duration, and the number of times I would sing about one hundred and ten, with seldom more than a weeks rest from rehearsal as well. But I wished for nothing more than to work in peace to the best of my ability.

One day I went into the stalls to hear a little of the rehearsal, and found Charles Lucas there. At that time he was Principal of the Royal Academy of Music, and a member of the firm Addison, Lucas and Hollier, publishers of LOVE'S TRIUMPH. 'Young man' he said, 'You have made a mistake in refusing the part; the opera will be the greatest success we have since THE BOHEMIAN GIRL'. I replied that in my opinion it would not be a success. He was angry that I disagreed with him, a man of such long and varied experience. He repeated: 'it will be an enormous success, and you will be sorry you did not take part in it".

SECOND EMPIRE OPERA by T.J. Walsh.

At the Theatre Lyrique in Paris early in 1864 Carvalho was endeavouring to mitigate his wife's absence from Paris stage by reaching an agreement with fellow director Halanzier whereby, for part of the Marseille season, her place would be taken by Marie Cabal. There is some evidence that a similar arrangement had been effected with the Lyons Opera. Coupled with a work of Balfe, a second Irish composer, Wallace, was having his opera LOVE'S TRIUMPH, which had lately been produced at Covent Garden, put forward for production at the Theatre Lyrique.

THE DESERT FLOWER

Text by A.J.Harris and T.J. Williams, based on the play by Vernoy de St. George and de Leaven, and made into the opera JAGUARITA D'INDI-ENNE by Halevy in Paris (1855).

First Production: 12th October 1863 at Covent Garden.
Other Production: New York on 15th January 1868

CHARACTERS;

Oanita (Desert Flower)	Soprano
Captain Maurice	Baritone
Maj. Hector Pumpernickel	Tenor
Cascan (Indian Chief)	Bass
Indian Maiden	Mezzo-Soprano
Sergeant Peterman	Tenor

121

"As a drama this piece is of French origin, being a version of the opera JAGUARITA D'INDIENNE, produced at the Theatre Lyrique, Paris, with music by Halevy some years ago. Its success was transient, being chiefly owing to the acting and singing of Madame Marie Cabal; certainly its merits are not such as to make it worthy of revival on the English stage, for the incidents are confused and improbable, and the story inspires but little interest... Our composers accept anything in the shape of a libretto that is put in their hands. Such a libretto may please for a time; the public may applaud fine songs, pretty dancing and showy spectacle; but they soon tire of such things when they are not combined with something better. There is not an instance to be found of a permanently successful opera not possessed of sterling dramatic as well as musical merit."

"We should only weary our readers by divulging the plot and incidents of such a piece as THE DESERT FLOWER, incidents drawn from Cooper's "Tales of American Life". The heroine, who bears the pretty subriquet Desert Flower, is the queen or chieftainess of a tribe of American Indians at war with the inhabitants of a European settlement. The Military Commander of the whites and the Indian Queen, happening to meet, are changed from enemies to lovers; and after a sufficiency of adventures and perils to liberty and life incurred for each other's sake, are married by way of denouement. This tender Dessert Flower is a regular savage, familiar with blood; she is accessible to female feelings only through the novel influence, for her, of love. She is an impossible personage, for a chieftainess of an American Indian tribe could not have existed among people whose women are among the most abject specimen of female humanity."

"But Miss Pyne, with versatile talent, looks and acts this truculent savage so cleverly, and sings with such remarkable brilliance, that all this absurdity passes off quite smoothly. The lover captain Maurice, as personated by Mr. Harrison, is a good-looking soldierly fellow, pleasant enough, but possessing of no quality which creates any serious interest. There is another person, Major Hector Pumpernickel, the buffo of the piece, whose only vocation is to make us laugh. Lastly, for the dramatis personae are fewer than usual, there is Cascan, an Indian Chief, the rejected lover of the Queen, and the villain of the story, a stalwart savage with a tremendous bass voice. Both these characters are well represented, the former by Mr. Corri, and the latter by Mr. Weiss."

"Such being the dramatic quality of the opera, it is easy to see that its success must mainly depend upon its music. In this respect it is entitled to much praise. Wallace's reputation is well established, and will be maintained by the music of THE DESERT FLOWER. We are not sure tht he has ever risen above the height of his first opera MARITANA, but with that exception, he has never written anything so uniformly good as this. It has all the freshness, vigour, grace and melody which abound in all Wallace's works; and it is written with even more than his usual correctness and purity of style. Like all our English operas, it contains many songs and ballads introduced less with a view to dramatic appropriateness than to popularity and profit as concert and drawing room morceaux; and in some of them this object has been successfully gained. Two songs in particular 'Why throbs this heart', sung by Miss Pyne, and 'Though born in woods' sung by Mr. Harrison, will soon be found on every piano in the kingdom."

"The opera, splendidly got up and admirable performed, was received by the densely crowded audience with warmest applause. We never heard Miss Pyne sing with greater brilliance and beauty. Mr. Harrison was also eminently successful, his voice being sweet and flexible. The whole performance was characterised by good taste and good judgement. Mr. Corri's comic singing was lively and agreeable; and Mr. Weiss's magnificent voice and musician-like execution were heard to great advantage. The only remaining part was given to Miss Susan Pyne, and is so insignificant as to be quite unworthy of that lady's talents. The choruses and morceaux d'ensemble were excellently sung; and the orchestra, under the direction of Mr. Mellon, maintained its characteristic power and efficiency."

Review from 'THE DAILY TELEGRAPH':
"The plot is a weak perversion of the narrative of Captain Smith and Pocohontas in the original story. The music is graceful and tuneful, its colouring being derived from the frequent repetition of a quaint Indian air, but it is not strongly original. It was a sumptuous production, and the band and chorus, under Mr. Alfred Mellon, sustained their well-earned reputation."

Light-hearted piece from 'Punch', 24 October 1863

"THE DESERT FLOWER is blooming in covent Garden, and the balmy airs which now float about the Opera House are already beginning to breathe their fragrance over the loud and soft pedals of the drawing room pianoforte. The Poetical and Romantic librettist have playfully adopted the word 'Desert' into the title, yet from the beginning of the opera to the end, there's nothing like a desert to be seen. Its a pretty name, so with fruit and flowers in abundance, what the juice more can be wanted ?.

BIBLIOGRAPHY

ARDITI, Luigi: 'Reminiscences
ARUNDEL, Dennis: 'The Critic at the Opera'
BERLIOZ, Hector: 'Les Soirees de l'Orchestre'
DENT, Edward J. : 'The Foundations of English Opera'
ELSON, Arthur : 'A Critical History of Opera'
FLOOD, W.H. Grattan: 'W.V. Wallace - a Memoir'
FORSYTH, Cecil : 'Music and Nationalism'
GALLOWAY, W. Johnson : 'The Operatic Problem'
GANZ, Wilheim : 'Memories of Musicians'
GRAVES, Perceval : ' The "Maritana" Wallace'
GROVE, G. : 'Dictionary of Music and Musicians'
KREHBIEL, Henry :   'A book of Operas'
                      'Golden Jubilee of New York Philharmonic
                      Symphonic Society Booklet'

KLEIN, Herman : 'The Golden Age of Opera'
KLEIN, J. W. : 'Wallace, a Reassessment' (Opera Magazine)
LEE, Ernst M. : 'The Story of Opera'
LOEWENBERG, Alfred : 'The Annals of Opera'
MAPLESON, James H. : 'The Mapleson Memoirs'
PLANCHE, J.R. : 'Recollections and Reflections'
REEVES, Sims, : 'Life and Recollections'
SHAW, G. B. : 'London Music in 1888-89' (Corno di Bassetto)
SAINTLY, Charles : 'Reminiscences
SCHOLES, Percy A. : 'Mirror of Music'
WALLACE, Carew V.: Letter from William V. Wallace Jnr.
WHITE, E.W. : 'The Rise of English Opera'
WYNDHAM, Henry S. : 'The Annals of Covent Garden'

Covent Garden Archives
'Brooklyn Review', New York
'Decies' Vol 35, W.S.E.A.S. Magazine
Freeman's Journal, Dublin (National Library)
Illustrated London News
'Message Bird' Newspaper, New York
Saunder's Newsletter, Dublin (National Library)
The Times, London
Waterford News (Waterford Municipal Library)